GRUMPY OLD WORKERS

Also by Stuart Prebble

Grumpy Old Men: The Official Handbook
Grumpy Old Men: The Secret Diary
Grumpy Old Christmas

STUART PREBBLE

Illustrations by Noel Ford

Weidenfeld & Nicolson
London

First published in Great Britain in 2007
by Weidenfeld & Nicolson

10 9 8 7 6 5 4 3 2 1

Text © Stuart Prebble 2007
Illustrations © Noel Ford 2007

ISBN 978 0 297 85362 6

Designed and typeset in ITC Charter by Geoff Green Book Design

Printed and bound in Great Britain by Mackays of Chatham plc, Chatham, Kent

Weidenfeld & Nicolson

The Orion Publishing Group Ltd
Orion House
5 Upper Saint Martin's Lane
London, WC2H 9EA
www.orionbooks.co.uk

The Orion Publishing Group's policy is to use papers that are natural, renewable and recyclable products and made from wood grown in sustainable forests. The logging and manufacturing processes are expected to conform to the environmental regulations of the country of origin.

For Alex

Everything in this book really happened. Some of the names have been changed to protect the innocent

Contents

Preface

A s our regular readers will know, I sometimes like to start with a mental picture of your good self as you are picking up and reading this book for the first time.

This was fairly easy to do in the case of *Grumpy Old Christmas*, because there was a strong likelihood that the book was being received as a Christmas present. We envisioned the recipient flicking through the first few pages, and trying to work out how to appear to be in good humour about the assumption that he was a grumpy old bastard who would find lots to enjoy in a book about how crap Christmas is. A tricky one, I think you'll agree, but I like to believe that between us we got through it fairly well.

It's a bit more difficult in this case but, for the first of what are bound to be several indulgences in the following pages, I'd like us to imagine that you are reading this on the bus, tube or train, on the way to work. And if you are in a car on the way to work, it's to be hoped that you are listening to the talking book or sitting in the back while your chauffeur does the driving. If you're reading and driving at the same time, I'm sure that's fine, but then just watch out for me as I go by on the pedestrian crossing just in front of you. No need to worry, obviously, about the lollipop lady.

If I'm right, and you are on your way to work, you could do this exercise with me. If I'm not, you could either read on and visualise this next bit, or you could stop reading and do something useful until you are next on your way to work. Up to you. I have no control over you ... obviously ...

Anyway, on your way to wherever you are going this morning, or tomorrow morning, or whatever, just pause to take a close look at the faces all around you. Look into the faces of the other commuters. On the bus. On the street. On the train. On the tube. On the pavement. In their cars. Just take a careful look.

Probably you don't want to stare too overtly, because round our way that could get you filled in, but see if you can have a good hard neb without the person you're looking at catching your eye.

It shouldn't be too difficult, because one thing you'll notice fairly quickly is that most people are gazing into space. What unoriginal novelists describe as 'staring into the middle distance', not focussed on anything in particular, just existing in a faint fug of semi-consciousness. Chances are that lots of the people you'll be looking at have ear-plugs or ear-speakers or whatever the hell they call the things that we used to assume meant that you were hard of hearing, and are listening to some noise which is not dissimilar to the racket that's going to be drilling into your skull for eternity after you die and go to hell for your sins.

A sea of faces, line upon line, like waves merging, all basically the same, and all ever-so-slightly different. After a while of doing this, by the way, I think you'll find that you start to wonder how it's possible for there to be so many different people, all with the same basic configuration of two eyes, a nose and a mouth, but all looking just slightly different from one another. All those millions of people, and all looking just very slightly different. Weird shit, huh?

Anyway, that's not why we're looking. We're looking to see if we can discover something about the world of work. Most of these people are on their way to work. On their way to do the thing they spend more of their time doing than anything else, other than sleeping. More, then, than anything else in their conscious life. Eight hours a day on average, plus anything up to another four hours or more for the commute. Maybe as much as twelve hours out of the twenty-four, five or more days a week, dedicated to the thing that enables us to pay the bills.

So since this is such an important part of our lives then, I guess we must all take enormous care about what we do – and that we're happy doing it. That must be right, yes?

Well, let's see if we can get a clue by looking at the faces. What do you see? Bright happy shiny people full of optimism and looking forward to the challenges and exhilaration of the day ahead? Does anyone see that at all? Some chance.

If you see the same thing that I see, you see a picture of despondence. A picture of despair, desperation and disillusion. You see crowds upon crowds of mostly pallid complexions which look as though they have never seen the sun. Or indeed black or brown faces of people whose ancestors probably saw a lot of sun, but who equally look as though they haven't been in daylight for the past decade. You see the faces of the walking dead. An animated Lowry.

What is that devastating line from Henry David Thoreau? 'Most men lead lives of quiet desperation and go to the grave with the song still in them.' People who look as though they have had their inner selves surgically removed with scalpels, whose blades have been tempered in the fires of hell. Vacant expressions on faces half-paralysed with inertia, unable and unwilling to react or respond in any way to what their senses are telling them about the world outside. A sort of half-life, neither fully asleep nor fully awake, existing in a twilight zone.

In fact it's not that they are failing to engage with the outside world. What they are actually engaged in is their daily struggle to keep the real world out for as long as possible – or at least until they get to work, at which point they probably have little choice but to sharpen up just a bit and do their level best to look as though they're part of the human family. Some more than others, it has to be said. Have you ordered a cup of coffee in Coffee Republic? They don't seem to bother at all.

What is this like? No, just think about it for a minute. What is this like? So far as most of us can be certain, we've all got just one life. It's not, as the ever-expanding posse of bores-for-England keep reminding us 'a dress rehearsal'. This is it. One chance. One go around. One life. 'Seize the day', and all that bollocks. And just look at us. Just look around. How are most of us spending it?

Sitting on the train, in the tube, on the bus etc etc for hour after hour after day after week after year, as our lives slip away – just so that we can work for most of our waking lives – for the man. Our precious lives slipping away like sand through a timer, and the size and shape of the kick we get out of that can be seen imprinted on all those faces.

So, life WAS a bloody dress rehearsal, after all!

And it's not just some of us, it's all of us. 'It may be the devil, or it may be the lord, but you're gonna have to serve somebody.' Isn't that what Dylan sang? 'You may be the ambassador to England or France ...' etc. No matter who you are, or where you are, you have to serve somebody.

When I first heard that, about 400 years ago, I knew it must be true of the waiter or the hospital porter. I've been both of those in my time, and I sure as hell had to serve somebody. But at that time I thought that actually it wouldn't be true if you were the Chief Executive. Well guess what, since then I've been the Chief Executive, and sure enough – just like the waiter and the hospital porter, you get to serve somebody.

You've got to serve somebody if you are the Queen of England or the Prime Minister. You've got to serve somebody if you are the President of Russia or the United States. What is more – and I think we can all take some comfort in this – you've got to serve somebody if you are the richest man in the world. Yes, it turns out that Bill Gates isn't able simply to hoard his billions and relax doing what the hell he likes. It seems as though he has a conscience that forces him to justify all that money – to try to buy the thing that all of the billions don't confer by right – the respect of the rest of us. So he's serving society's expectations that rich men will do philanthropic works. Good for him, we all say, and especially good for him that he's the richest man in the world, and he still has to serve somebody.

All of which is a long way around of saying that this book is for everybody. This book is for the GPs, the JPs, the MPs and the VIPs. The masters, the servants, the slaves. It's about the world of work and all its evil deeds, and it turns out that in some way or another everybody has to do it. So don't be surprised if you see Bill Gates buying this book at a news-stand. And if you do, just make sure the little fucker isn't stealing it – because I've got a living to make.

The Origin of the Species

So then, what is going to be our take on the world of work which isn't more than adequately covered by all those hundreds of volumes dedicated to it and cluttering up the shelves in your local library or bookshop? And why oh why would anyone want to buy and read a book about work in the first place? Surely it's bad enough to have to do it, without actually having to read about it?

The answer, we hope, is that as with every other important aspect of modern life, the 'Grumpy' point of view can give us a new perspective on something we have habitually regarded as a commonplace.

Yes, that's our job. To provide an interesting and, hopefully, entertaining new perspective on a lot of otherwise familiar stuff. We're allowed to hope that it'll be entertaining rather than just a load of whining because Grumpiness, as all true Grumpy Old Men and Women know, is not about being grumpy. It's not even about being miserable or unhappy.

It's a surprising fact, but by and large we're not.

Grumpiness is a way of looking at the world. A prism through which all the ultimately absurd bloody nonsense which dogs our everyday lives, hour by hour and minute by minute, can more healthily be viewed. In a nutshell, it identifies, names and shames all of the bollocks we have to put up with, sometimes at a distance of more than 1,000 yards. (Yes, I meant yards and not metres.)

So how and where did the Grumpy phenomenon begin?

There can be little doubt that Grumpiness itself has existed for a very long time; obviously at least as far back as the era of Snow White, the technical term for which, I believe, is the days of yore. But I think that in all modesty I can lay claim to be the first to have identified Grumpiness as a clinical syndrome.

What happened was that I was flicking through the pages of the *Daily Telegraph* at home, and came across an article which said something like '*35–54 year old men are the grumpiest in Britain*'. As I was about fifty at the time I read on with something as close to interest as I can usually summon when reading the daily paper.

The article was reporting the results of a survey which had been designed to try to discover which demographic group was the most cynical, the most depressed, the most generally pessimistic and pissed off. God knows who wanted to pay for a survey like that, but evidently someone did. They had asked a whole range of questions such as 'Do you think the world is a better place than when you were a child?', 'Do you think the NHS is improving?' and (good one this) 'Do you think that our leaders know better than we do?' Blimey.

They had obviously received the whole range of replies to their idiot questions, but when they did their little analysis at the end of the questionnaires, it turned out that this middle-aged group of men answered with the most negatives. 35–54 year old men. The grumpiest age and gender in Britain.

Being, at the time, right in the core of this group, I of course recognised the phenomenon. I fitted the description to a T (whatever that means). I was grumpy. Grumpy about the telly, grumpy about everything to do with travelling, grumpy about other people, grumpy about mobile phones, grumpy about supermarkets, queuing, airports, grumpy about newspapers and the radio. Well, you get the idea – just about everything pissed me off.

Up until then, I had assumed that it was just me. That I was the only person going around the place with a continual running commentary inside my head: 'Why has that bloke got a question mark strapped around his ear?', and 'When did it become alright to record my conversation "for training purposes"?' Sure I occasionally used to worry that maybe I was going a bit crazy: since the Old Testament times, hearing voices hasn't necessarily been thought of as a good thing. But it wasn't like I was hearing these voices out loud, and it wasn't as though they were telling me to start walking around with a billboard around my neck. Certainly they occasionally told me to pick up an uzi and climb to the top of the tower, but as I seldom felt in much danger of giving in to the urge (other than when I saw John McCririck, obviously), I thought that my little inner voices were just the burden I had to live with.

So having read the results of the survey, I started to wonder, and I began to ask all my mates of about the same age as me whether they felt that they were grumpy. 'Of course,' they replied, almost to a man, 'given the state of the world, how the hell could anybody be anything else?' Or words to that effect.

I began to wonder why this might be. Why it is that apparently the 35–54 year old age group of men were the grumpiest, and not so much the older people, and not so much the younger people?

Traditionally we would have associated grumpiness with older people, by which I obviously mean *even*-older people. The term Grumpy Old Men would ordinarily have been thought to apply to ageing dribbling old gits sitting on park benches complaining that 'it wasn't like this when we were young'. But, surprise surprise, according to this survey, this older group was generally markedly happier than their middle-aged children. (And why, by the way, is there no word in English meaning 'grown-up children'? – that's another bloody irritation.)

Apparently, grumpiness had skipped a generation.

After a while and a lot of talking to people, I started to attach some logic to this phenomenon, and I have come to believe that the hare-brained nonsense I came up with must have some validity because over the years it has turned into a theory, and then into a number of TV series, and then into several books, a stage show, and a small industry. Yes, what started as a chronic state of getting-more-hacked-off-as-every-day-goes-by has now become a franchise.

It goes like this.

Grumpy Old Men grew up believing that the world was going to be a better place. Mostly we grew up in the sixties or the seventies – pre-Thatcherite Britain. It was a time of social revolution – or as near to social revolution as we were going to get – this is, after all, only Britain. We're not France, for heaven's sake. We believed in love and peace and harmony and quite a lot of free sex. Actually, having asked around about this too, I have discovered to my great relief that there wasn't quite as much free sex around as we might have been led to believe, but that's by the by. Probably a hangover from post-war rationing.

The point is that our parents and grandparents had survived two world wars, and therefore carried all the heavy baggage that inevitably goes with personal tragedy and loss and deprivation, and that's not to mention being woken up every night to the sound of sirens. But instead of making them grumpy, with only a small number of exceptions, it made them grateful to have lived when so many others had died. And it also made them feel the need to act responsibly, feed and clothe the family, and take an annual holiday in Benidorm if they could get a couple of weeks off in the summer. Limited expectations in a land fit for heroes etc etc. Far from being grumpy, they were relatively cheerful. Modest aspirations, easily fulfilled.

Our kids, on the other hand, didn't have any memory of post-war rationing, missed out on the liberation afforded by the contraceptive pill, didn't have the Vietnam war to react against, and were not the first people to discover starvation in Africa. They didn't have parents who were going to over-react to an eccentric haircut and in fact, because their parents were ageing hippies, they didn't have much else to rebel against at all. So the result seems to be that by and large they don't care about anything. They're not overly cheerful, it seems to us, and they're not overly grumpy either. They're more or less acquiescent, and that's another thing that makes Grumpy Old Men grumpy. That kids aren't angry. Because that's part of their job; kids are supposed to be angry. But again, that's another story.

So that just leaves us then. 35–54 years old, or thereabouts, and pissed off. And if you can identify with this and you are a little younger, or you can identify with all this and are a little older, take heart and remember. It's totally cool to be grumpy.

Grumpiness turns out to be both the blessing and the curse of those thus afflicted. The blessing is that we feel liberated about being able to recognise bullshit for what it is and for the most part being able to get a reasonable perspective on it; the curse is that we seem to be doomed to see contradiction, nonsense and sheer bollocks in every person and every place we look, and simply cannot prevent ourselves from asking questions about things that everyone else in the world seems to find obvious and acceptable.

What sort of thing am I talking about? Well of course, we're spoiled for choice, but how about this? It's a little thing, sure, but it's an illustration.

Today I was walking down the corridor of our office building when I came to a narrow part, and the young bloke who does general odd-jobs around the place was walking towards me from the other direction. Actually in our business, for some reason, we call this function a 'runner'. It eludes me why this should be, because I've never seen this bloke run, and I never expect to see this bloke run. Nor have I ever seen any of his colleagues in any situation run. Actually I'd be less surprised to see my daughter's pet goldfish break into a fast trot than I would be to see one of these blokes running, but that's by the by. And the question of what his job is called isn't the point of the story.

No, the point of the story is that this runner rather courteously stopped at this narrow part of the corridor to let me continue my way uninterrupted. Part of me likes this because it shows that he has some respect for his elders, but another part of me resents the fact that he obviously thinks I'm too fat to be passed in this part of the corridor, which is narrow but not all that narrow. Also indeed, that he plainly thinks that I am so decrepit that I need to be given leeway, rather in the way that I will usually give a wide berth to an octogenarian or someone with a zimmer. Again, all good fodder for further grumpiness, but still not the point.

Let's get to it, at last, shall we? To the question that Grumpies ask but which seems not to occur to everyone else. Being as how he had stopped, even though I hadn't asked him to and wasn't sure how I felt about it, I naturally said 'thank you' and quick as a flash he responded with the words 'no worries'. And so here is the question that Grumpies would ask which everyone else would seem apparently to find obvious.

What does that mean?

'No worries'? 'No worries'? Why does this bloke think it's necessary to tell me that there are 'no worries' about the fact that he has paused momentarily in *his* stride to let me go by without breaking *my* stride? Why does he need to reassure me of that? It would never occur to me in a million years that there were any worries. Why would anybody worry about that? So I really don't need to be assured that there aren't any.

Even I am not so sheltered that I don't know that this is an Australian version of the phrase 'no problem', but this in itself defeats me. If someone had told me a few years ago that this utterly naff Australian expression would become current in Britain, I would have laughed until my head burst. These people have done for the English language what Dr Harold Shipman did for the red Ford Espace. All my instincts are that we would be about as attracted to the idea of emulating their way of speaking as we would be to stepping in a three-week-old turd – with bare feet.

If this bloke had said 'not a problem' – which seems to be in equally common modern parlance – I would have thought it was bad enough. How could it cause a problem to lose half a second while I go by? But please, not 'no worries'? What on earth ...?

Want another one? Another example of questions that pop into the minds of Grumpy Old Men that don't seem to occur to normal people? Probably not but I'm on a roll here, so maybe just a quickie.

How is it legal to advertise a help-line phone number but not to employ anyone to answer the phone? No really. How can it be OK to cause other members of the human race all the irritation, annoyance and bad temper that inevitably arise from doing that? See what I mean? Obvious to everyone else, apparently, but not at all obvious to Grumpies.

What do people mean when they say they've called or emailed me just to 'touch base'? Does that mean they have something to say but didn't say it? Or that they don't have anything to say but wanted to remind me that they're alive? I guess it's just another of those word things, but it irritates me. And there are ten thousand more.

So there we are. We're Grumpy. Grumpy Old Men and Grumpy Old Women. We probably aren't going to fight back because we can't be arsed. We probably aren't going to write to our MPs because they're more useless than the people we're complaining about. We probably aren't going to take to the streets because we did that all those years ago about Vietnam and rather fewer years ago about Iraq, and look what good it did us.

But we are going to point it out. And we're going to be angry. And then when we're done being angry we're going to be tetchy, and then we're going to cry, and finally we're going to laugh. All of which taken together adds up, in the way we have now defined it, as 'Grumpy'. We're Grumpy, and who in their right mind would be otherwise?

No no, we're not going to do anything useful, but equally we're not going to suffer in silence. We used to. We used to sit and read or watch the various symptoms of the fact that our world has been taken over by officious arseholes, and just mumble or mutter or look skywards and tut. But then along came 'Grumpiness'. Grumpy Old Men and Grumpy Old Women. Yes that's right, we've made it OK to be grumpy.

We've made it OK to point out that the only reason that this two-lane road has now been narrowed by a huge bulge in the pavement so that you have to wait for ten minutes for a pause in the oncoming traffic, is because there is some lame brain in an office trying to spend his budget and justify his continued existence. Rather good to state loudly and frankly that 'your call is important to us' simply cannot be true because if it was you would answer the sodding phone. Very commendable to point out to the bank manager that charging us £40 to send us a letter telling us that we are 26p in the red is not OK, and that we want it refunded or we'll take you to court.

Phew. Got a bit hot and bothered there. Sorry. Let's calm down and think for a minute. Oh yes. We're Grumpy. Grumpy about everything in general, but in this volume we're Grumpy about work in particular.

As I mentioned earlier, I've been a waiter and I've been the waited upon, I've been the hospital porter and I've been Chief Executive, so that in the following pages I hope we can get a little perspective on all of them.

So then, what is our plan? Well I think what we'll do is to see if we can distil the Grumpy's experience of work into a chronology which you might find useful when working out how to get a job, keep a job or cope with losing a job. Some of it might be helpful if you are a sort of apprentice Grumpy and need a few tips on how to cope with all the bollocks that employment has to throw at you. Some of it may be good advice if you are not a Grumpy at all, but have to deal with Grumpies in the course of pursuing your chosen career.

Along the way we might bump into some personal reminiscences derived from a lifetime of being vexed, irritated, and generally pissed about in the workplace. So that if, like me, you are a fully fledged Grumpy, you might recognise a few things along the way. And if in the course of doing so we can add a sometimes entertaining perspective to the daily grind that seems to be the lot of all of us, then our day will not have been entirely wasted. I suppose.

Junior School Expectations

So that's how Grumpy Old Men and Women got to be so grumpy about the world in general, but how did we get to be as jaundiced, cynical, disenchanted and generally hacked off about the world of work in particular? Because it seems that the wide world of work introduces a whole new dimension to our grumpiness.

Getting a job, starting a job, commuting to a job, doing a job, trying to get along in a job, surviving a job and leaving a job – voluntarily or otherwise – are all sources of considerable vexation, and none of that is to mention all the stuff in between.

Well, as with every other aspect of Grumpiness, our grumpiness about work derives from the triumph of disappointment over expectation. Grumpy is what we become when our hopes and expectations are disappointed. When the warm and balmy dreams of the summer days of our youth are confronted by the icy blast of the reality of the modern world. And so to get to the bottom of how our youthful hopes and dreams about work were shattered, I found myself wondering about the first impressions we gained as kids about what the whole experience of work was going to be like.

One of the rare treats enjoyed by Grumpy Old Men and Women when we were at junior school was the occasional film show. Does anyone remember that? We would be summoned to the hall by the sound of classical music played on a wind-up gramophone with one of those speakers that looked like an ancient ear-trumpet. You remember, His Master's Voice, and you expected to see a puppy sitting underneath. A lovely big black shiny flat disc with a label in the middle going around at seventy-eight revolutions per minute. That's a lot of revolutions.

A needle on the end of an electronic arm scraping along inside the parallel grooves like an ice-skater. A few seconds of noisy grainy static before the first bars of music emerged. The arm holding the needle bobbing up and down alarmingly as it struggled to stay in the groove. Everyone had to tiptoe around it for fear of the needle jumping out and slewing across the record with a sickening screech, and thereby ruining it for ever in an instant.

Does anyone remember a natty little drawer somewhere on those old machines which contained the replacement needles? You'd unscrew a little wheel holding the present one in, and carefully replace it with a nice new one. Everything would sound crisp and clear for about five minutes before something else happened to damage the new needle and it needed to be replaced again. We're talking well before the 'stylus', which was a whole other thing.

Resonating out of this ear-trumpet there came forth a tinny but wonderfully evocative sound that you can still hear every bit as clearly in your head today, echoing around from the deep recesses of your mental hard-drive across time and space from maybe forty-odd years ago. In our case the regular music of choice was what I learned later was a background melody to 'Jesu joy of man's desiring', and every time I have ever heard that particular piece of music from that day to this I instantly smell the smell of stale cabbage and floor polish in my nostrils and I'm back in short trousers and wearing a tie that I didn't know how to tie.

At the sound of the music bouncing off walls, all glossed in green and cream paint, and reverberating around the corridors, everyone in the school would form into their snakes, in pairs, excruciatingly embarrassed to be holding hands with the girl next to you, and proceed to the hall. For some reason I had been paired off with Diane Tyler, whose hands were always sticky from constantly carrying around the contraband sweets which were a form of currency in the playground. Do you remember all that? Flying saucers? Sherbet dips? All sorts of all sorts.

Once in the hall we would sit crossed-legged on the floor, in our rows, the youngest at the front, the middle ones in the middle and the oldest at the back sitting on long benches which we called 'forms'. I reckon there were about 150 of us.

The school hall was just a big empty room with walls covered by paintings and projects, most of them about outer space or the pyramids, and with no furniture other than a few bench seats around the edges. There was also the nature table, which exhibited a motley collection of fir cones, acorns, conkers, dried leaves, eye of newt and tongue of toad, and rotting bark from trees of types and varieties which did not exist within twenty miles of West Norwood. The closest we got to nature round our way was the occasional squashed hedgehog in the middle of the road, the fascination of its bloody assortment of mushed-up guts and spines luring us into the path of a further accident.

In the middle of the hall, standing high up on a plinth like a primitive icon, there was a bloody great machine which turned out to be a film projector, its many wheels and cogs and moving parts painted in mottled metallic grey. A worthy object of worship for impressionable and tiny kids.

The film itself was wound up tightly on a big reel hoisted up above it by a tapered metal arm. For some reason I could never fathom, it seemed that none of the teachers was quite able to master what now seems to me to be the rather simple task of threading the 16mm film through the little pathways of cogs and sprockets, passing in between the projected light and the lens, and then out the other side to be collected on a revolving reel at the bottom. Somehow or other the film always took a wrong turn along its prescribed route, turning anti-clockwise around a wheel around which it should have turned clockwise (if you see what I mean). Or the tension was too loose, or the tension was too tight. Certainly the tension was fairly intense on the many occasions that the thing ground to a sickening halt with the air filling with the unmistakeable smell of burning celluloid.

Everyone from that generation can still recall the particular clickety click of the electric motor and see the flickering light on the screen. The hall had very effective black-out blinds, presumably left over from the war, which used to render the whole room into more or less total darkness – which always set everyone off giggling with a mix of nervousness and anticipation. Roderick Laylor would take the opportunity for a quick tug on the pigtails of Carol Hastie, whom he teased without charm or mercy but on whom he undoubtedly had a very precocious crush. Even pre-pubescent, Roderick was a little bit of a wanker.

These few moments of complete darkness also provided the cover for a range of other sins and iniquities such as the passing of idiotic notes of the 'you stink' variety, and the exchange of any 'class A' drugs that were then in fashion. Got your attention? Just seeing if you were still awake. The closest we got to 'class A' drugs in those days was a Wagon Wheel.

This was well before anyone had discovered anything as mundane and irritating as health and safety, so that in what must have been the rather likely event of a fire, no-one would have known the way to the exits. In those innocent days, before negligent teachers who killed children in their charge would face the consequence of being paraded on the front pages of the tabloids, our teachers welcomed this as a chance for an hour or so of peace and quiet. A chance for them to nip out into the playground for a swift drag on a Consulate, and God knows what else.

The head teacher, Mr Spanner (anyone remember him? the bloke with halitosis?), would give us a little introductory talk along the lines of how lucky we were to have the chance to see films during school hours, and how he would have given his right arm to have had such a treat when he was at school. I remember we thought that this was a particularly vivid and unfortunate reference because, of course, the class 3 teacher Mr Pottinger had at some time in the past indeed given his right arm. Though not, I was later assured by my father, for the sake of being allowed to see a film.

Anyway, I guess these films must have been made by whatever was the contemporary euphemism for the Ministry of Truth. Mostly they were propaganda of one kind or another, about the upcoming 11+ and the virtues of the different types of education available to us thereafter. I remember that all of us wanted to be sure to fail the 11+ because the prospect of doing all that wood-work and sport looked so much more fun than all those creepy and pallid-looking kids with the centre partings doing Latin.

From its standing start with a cross on the screen, the reel would run down through the lens, 8–7–6–5–4–3, and then nothing until the first picture. The sound would crackle into life from a small box at the front of the class. Fanfare, title caption, and off we would go.

I remember one of these films in particular which caught my imagination because it was about what life would be like in the 21st century. I well recall wondering why anyone would bother to tell us what life would be like in forty years because by that time we would be about fifty years old, and surely therefore we would all be dead? And if not, we'd be as close to it as made no difference. Certainly in the wholly unlikely event that one might still be alive by the age of sixty, we would be just an embarrassment to ourselves and everyone else. That was even older than my parents, for heaven's sake, and they were fossils in their early thirties.

Anyway, this film was about the future and what life would be like when we had mechanised the world. Robots would be doing all our everyday chores, highly automated production lines would mean human beings didn't have to do any heavy lifting, and very complex-looking adding machines would be doing all our arithmetic for us. Even then I didn't really know why grownups seemed to have to do so much arithmetic, and it was an almighty relief to know that I might not need to bother.

If I'm honest, I can't remember if it was in this film, or maybe in something even more futuristic that I saw in the cinema, but I do remember being particularly impressed by the way we would all travel to work. You must have seen this, and it certainly came up in the first programmes in the Grumpy Old Men cannon. You'd get into a little capsule and be whisked through one of a large number of interlinking perspex tubes which wove their way high in the sky above the skyscrapers. A bit like the systems they used to have in a few department stores where your money whooshed off in a little pod to some central accounts area, and after a few minutes your change and a receipt whooshed back.

I don't think that film-makers had the technology then to actually enable us to see a moving representation of this exciting prospect in action, and more probably I'm remembering a series of stills from a comic strip or something, but it did genuinely involve happy smiling people, faces aglow with enthusiasm, shooting backwards and forwards, their route uninterrupted by anything as irritating as a speed bump in the road, and certainly not by any other pods. Or squashed hedgehogs.

Everyone in these pictures seemed to be wearing a sort of tunic of the kind you'd probably associate with the barber, and in what I'm guessing would have been (if we had only had colour in those days) a range of pastel shades. Once at their destination, our shiny people with their shiny teeth and very shiny and tightly controlled hair would emerge from their pods and go to sit in front of some impossibly futuristic piece of machinery, which was whirring away, performing some undefined function or other. This was even before the whirling reel-to-reel wheels of prehistoric computers.

Breakfast in these households of the future consisted of a pill and a glass of some wonder energy drink or other, lunch would be some more pills, and dinner was, can you guess it? Yes, that's right, more pills. In those days we certainly didn't anticipate that the future would involve Jamie fucking Oliver. With their lumpy mashed potato, cold prunes and watery custard, and the occasional slab of liver with sinews running through it, our school dinners were shitty enough as it was, without him getting involved with them.

But the key point was that all of the automation and technology had taken the drudgery and back-breaking toil out of work. So many machines were doing so many things for us that people would only need to work for a few hours a week, if that. And when we got home, robots and automatons would be doing the laundry and the vacuuming and making ready the vitamin-balanced pills. Progress and technology would produce a world of leisure and luxury, in which life could be lived in what seemed to be calm and harmony. Certainly these films did not address anything as inconvenient as how we might fairly distribute all of the wealth and largesse which would be ours, apparently with so very little effort.

OK, so in case you are not feeling spellbound by this wonderful jaunt into the middle of the last century, and are wondering why we're going on at such length in a book about work, we'll come to the point. It is herein where lies the root of the Grumpiness that many of us feel about the world of work.

Because this is what we were told it was going to be like. Sterile people in a sterile world of efficiency, calmness, apparent equality, and lots of time-off to play.

Sure, sterile isn't fun, but these were the days before we realised that sterile wasn't fun. This just looked great to us. We were Dan Dare. Fireball XL5 come to life. We just couldn't wait to grow up and get into Lady Penelope and drive a sleek, pink, tail-finned car with a glass bubble over our heads.

So how did all that go then? How has all that worked out? Well, we reflected a bit about this in the introduction, and I reckon that the expressions on the faces of real people going to and from real work in the real 21st century tell us everything we need to know about what became of that optimistic vision from nearly fifty years ago.

The short answer is that, indeed, the world of work is run by bloody automatons, but the cruel twist in this otherwise fairytale story is that the bloody automatons are us.

Before we get going on all that, though, let's concentrate on this business of how we are travelling to work in the first place. What happened to the dream of all those glistening, air-cushioned, automated pods whooshing us without hesitation or deviation in just a minute or two towards our destinations? Is that how it turned out? Any hands up at the back of the class? I think you've probably got it.

Our real-life journey to work in the real-life 21st century begins as we drag ourselves out of the house directly into the pouring rain, and walk along a pavement covered in spit, squashed chewing gum, dog-shit and the occasional used condom. We are bombarded on all sides by hoardings advertising unfamiliar stuff, and we don't know what it is, and we don't know what it does. We have to try to avoid walking near the gutter because chances are a bloke in a white van will think it's amusing to screech by as close as possible so that a tidal wave of dirty rainwater will spoil our otherwise carefree morning. We'll have to dodge and weave along the pavement to avoid having an eye poked out by the sharp end of a spoke from an open umbrella, wielded by someone who plainly doesn't give a damn if he or she blinds us or not. This won't be easy because, in addition to the crowds of commuters, large groups of schoolgirls will be standing across the whole pathway, chatting about the size of Damian's willy, or what Errol did to Tanya last night, and in the process blocking our onwards route. Or maybe half a dozen of them, also usually girls, will be walking along arm in arm, apparently oblivious to the idea that you exist at all, which of course, to them, you don't.

You blunder on through the wind and rain for maybe half a mile in order to arrive at a specified point where you get to wait in a long line of people and where, if we are lucky, a bus may occasionally deign to stop. Sometimes even to pick up passengers as well as to let them off. The magical RTs and RTLs and Routemasters, with the cheerful conductor leaping up and down the stairs and rattling his bag of coins, have gone the way of all good things. I loved the little machine that was strapped to his front and always wanted to be allowed to turn the little handle which produced the bus ticket. Chances are these days that our bus is going to be one of those articulated things which seem like two buses precariously joined together by a piece of rubber in the middle, and which appear to have the sole purpose of squashing cyclists caught on the inside of the bend.

While we wait, we may well have the opportunity to experience the additional joy of standing on piles of shattered glass because the bus shelter has been vandalised overnight. Just next to us, we get to admire the artistic efforts of some of our neighbours declaiming which gang happens to be predominant around this area, and into which of Myleen's various orifices Jos would like to insert his 'knob'. Some poor sod whose head is somewhere in la-la land and is currently enjoying the benefits of what I believe is called 'care in the community' is walking around and around the same lamp-post that he'll still be walking around when we get off the bus in ten hours from now. In fact his day may well turn out to be remarkably similar to our own.

At last, in the far distance, we might spy a bus approaching, but as it gets closer we see that it's being driven by someone who looks as though he may be casting for a part in the bar scene of the next *Star Trek* movie. Despite the fact that you and/or everyone else around you are frantically waving your arms, three or four buses thus driven by extra-terrestrials will sail by. Eventually, however, if you are lucky, one will stop at your bus stop. To be more precise, it'll actually stop just about three yards from the pavement, so that you are obliged to walk ankle deep through a muddy puddle if you are to get on. The queue will surge forward.

At this point, we will be the idiot who stops to help the nice Chinese lady on with her push-chair and everyone else will take the opportunity to bundle past us, probably presuming that we are a paedophile. By the time the nice Chinese lady and her offspring are on the bus, the driver will declare that it is full and that we'll have to wait for the next one. Just when we are on the point of persuading ourselves of the wisdom of going back home to spend the rest of the day in bed, chances are that another full bus will come along, followed immediately by an empty one, and we can continue our journey to the underground.

I think we'll save our description of the underground for another day, because even I am losing the will to live, and all this is before we even reach the place where we are supposed to do our jobs.

So all that was a generalised rant about the treachery perpetrated on us about the commute. The really important way in which we were misled as kids by all those films that gazed into the Elysium which was to be our future, was about the nature of the work itself.

Do you remember those scenes of people at work? There was always just the faintest hum of huge power in the background. There would be rows of metal cabinets with rows of dials and rows of lights, flashing in random sequences. Men in clean overalls and carrying clipboards would walk casually along, checking read-outs, nodding their heads and making their notes. There was no sign of any of the people who used to do by hand what all these machines now did automatically, and nor did it occur to any of us to ask what had become of them. If anyone thought about it at all, presumably the people who previously had undertaken all this work by manual labour were left with simple supervisory tasks. The only remaining problem facing them would be what to do with their vastly increased leisure time.

Of course this proposition relied on the rather naïve notion that, with all this extra kit and productivity, we would only want to make the same amount of stuff as we made before, so that the rest would be free time. All the work that human labourers used to take all day to do would have been achieved in a couple of hours using the machines. So presumably we'd just switch them off and take the rest of the afternoon as leisure? Perhaps a picnic by the river or a spot of croquet? More probably, according to the future-gazers, a 3D movie with glorious Sensurround and an energy-giving vitamin beverage served to us by people who looked like air-stewardesses. I'm not sure we'd thought all that out sufficiently clearly.

Quite how the makers of all those films arrived at the simple theory that the increased productivity made available by automation would be translated into free time, which would then be spread evenly among the workforce, must remain a mystery. Maybe they were idealists. Maybe they were communists. More probably, they were simply in the pay of Big Brother because, if anyone had realised what would be the actual consequences of all this exciting stuff, we would of course have rioted.

Because that's not what happened at all, was it? What happened was that instead of working for eight, ten, or twelve hours a day, which is probably the maximum any decent manual labourer could work, these machines could work for twenty-four hours a day. But since these wonderful new machines had cost so much to build and install, their owner had to get his investment back somehow. So they had to be put to maximum use. There wasn't going to be any question of producing in a few hours what we used to produce in many hours and then stopping. Obviously we were going to produce more stuff. More and more and more and more.

Thus several generations of workers whose job it used to be to do the actual work, but who used to stop at the end of an average working day, were now required to stand next to the thing that did the work. But instead of switching it off at the end of the average working day, this machine needed to work all through the night as well, and so someone had to stand next to it. And also through the weekend and through bank holidays, in order to maintain the mighty machines which had replaced the interesting part of what they used to do.

The bloke who used to be one of ten people fitting the rivets or whatever at the Ford factory at Dagenham now stood by on his own and watched as a robot placed the rivets at ten times the previous speed. Leaving nine other blokes with nothing to do, and one bloke still in a job. The bloke who used to hand-craft the individual leather seats in the Austin Morris factory got to witness a machine plumping and brushing or whatever you do with hand-tooled leather seats, while the rest of the human 'hands' were told to bugger off and not come back.

And of course the bloke who used to be able to down tools and stop the production line if he didn't like the fact that half the

workforce had been sacked and the other half were working themselves to death, could now sod off altogether and a scab supervisor could do his job and never notice his absence.

It wasn't just about machines either. Exactly the same thing happened in shops and offices and service industries and everywhere else. Fewer people working, but those that were working, were working much longer hours.

To be fair, not all of this happened overnight. It has to be said that there was a long period when it took one bloke to run the machine, and the other nine blokes sat around reading the newspaper. We will speak more of such things later, but then along came Mrs Thatcher to sort it out. And boy did she sort it out.

She brought along an era of unprecedented prosperity for those in certain types of work, while three and a half million people were thrown out of a job altogether. She made it OK for the

Gordon Gekko types in Wall Street to tell us that 'greed is good', while once-proud coal-miners and shipbuilders got drunk on street corners or played bingo. She made sure that the 'haves' had so much more, while the 'have nots' had even less.

Far from whatever extra leisure time and extra prosperity had been made available being spread evenly across the available workforce, what happened was that some of us got to work twelve or fourteen or sixteen hours a day and do well, and the rest got to lose our jobs altogether. The gap between rich and poor, I heard on the radio this very morning, is now wider than it has been for forty years. And, said this official report, the richest are not happy because they don't have anything to do with the poorest, and so don't really know that they are well off!

Miraculously, the revolution in automation that we were promised would turn our lives into a sort of gentle paradise on earth, actually turned into shit of one sort or another for just about everybody.

Excellent.

So by the time we got to our Grumpy years, Grumpy Old Men and Grumpy Old Women had witnessed this whole cycle. Huge and high expectations had been planted into our brain as kids, but by the time it came for delivery, what we actually got was a daft old cow with a big handbag.

It hasn't turned out as we were told it would turn out, and it never will turn out like that. And so we – who had been promised and had hoped for so much – are Grumpy. Grumpy Old Men and Grumpy Old Women. Doomed to put up with the shit we are in part responsible for having created – and just trying to see the funny side as an alternative to blowing our own brains out.

A Portrait of the Artist as a Young Grump

So then before we press on very much further, I thought we might explore a few aspects of the relationship of Grumpiness to work and, in particular, that we might try to answer one of the questions which scholars have been asking since the dawn of the industrial revolution. Specifically I mean the question of whether it is the grumpiness of Grumpy Old Men and Women that contributes to our overall jaundiced view of the world of work. Or is there inherent in the world of work the seeds of our grumpiness? The chicken and egg question.

To try to get to the root of this difficult philosophical conundrum, I thought we might take one of our little jaunts down memory terrace to see what there may have been in our early experience of work to have sewn the seeds of our grumpiness.

Having worked for about thirty years in various jobs in the area of broadcasting, I reckon that I've accumulated my share and several other people's of the sort of total bollocks which might well make one grumpy, and we'll come to some of that later on.

However, inevitably broadcasting yields only a certain kind of old bollocks. Different jobs and different walks of life no doubt throw up a whole range of bullshit of various hues and textures that makes the average sensible person of a certain age grumpy.

So I thought it might be fun and interesting to recall some of the other types of work I've experienced along my route towards quintessential Grumpidom. And if 'fun' and 'interesting' are too ambitious as targets, then maybe at least we might aspire towards interesting, as we remind ourselves what life was like in those simpler days when today's Grumps were in their apprenticeships. And if it turns out to be neither fun nor interesting, you could always just skip ahead to the next chapter, although if you find yourself doing that too often, you may feel that there is a risk that you get to the end of the book without getting your money's worth, and that would never do.

First impression: the paper-round

Like every other working-class kid before and probably since, my first job was as a paper-boy for the local newsagent. You probably had one too; do you remember? It involved getting up at 5.30 in the morning, probably six mornings a week, light or dark, summer and winter, rain or shine.

It was at the beginning of the 1960s, but boy were the sixties a long way off. Much more Vera Lynn and Vera Drake than Varoomshka and Van Morrison. It was pre-colour in every sense, with most of the memories of a childhood growing up in West Norwood in sepia.

I shared a small bedroom with my brother and both of us had paper-rounds, so both of us used to go through the same morning ritual. We had one of those wind-up clockwork alarms with a very loud tick which you told yourself you had to ignore, otherwise there was no chance of getting off to sleep. But of course the harder you tried to ignore it, the less likely you were to be able to do so. It had two large bells on the top with a hammer which used to vibrate between them, and boy oh boy was this no way to wake up in the morning. The sound was enough to summon extras from Michael Jackson's cemetery, and then the ferocity of the vibration would set the whole thing off travelling across the bed-side table so that it threatened to crash still more loudly onto the linoleum floor.

One of us had to turn it off in seconds for fear of waking up the aged Ps – both of whom, despite claiming to have slept through the early years of the Blitz, by then seemed liable to be awoken by a falling pin. Anyway, all of this worry about getting up on time militated against getting any decent sleep at all. This was no doubt all good training in sleep deprivation which left me with chronic insomnia later in life. In those days I was constantly yawning.

Though of course we know that the summers were longer and the beer was stronger in those days, it seems to me on recall that the rain was constantly lashing against the window on those early mornings, and the wind was perpetually howling between the three-storey blocks and turning the dustbin lids into lethal frisbees.

I'm sure we must have had some kind of heating in the flat, but if we did it certainly wasn't switched on yet, and the first dread of the day was the sensation of the freezing cold cotton of your shirt against goose-pimply skin. These were in the days before I had a satisfactory layer of blubber to protect me against the worst rigours of the cold.

I recall a thin mustard-coloured anorak – this was well before the advent of 'North Face' or any of those very clever insulating materials – which was as windproof as muslin and as waterproof as blotting paper. It never seemed to have fully dried out from the day before. Also a pair of woollen gloves, which had been knitted by a well-intentioned aunt but had not survived the wear and tear of the job in hand, and so had holes at the ends of each of the fingers. My brother and I each had a woolly home-knitted scarf, and we would experiment with different configurations of tucking them around our necks and heads, the favoured arrangement involving a final loop across the mouth so that our own warm breath would be reflected back into our faces.

This unhappy picture was finished off by a bobble-hat – predecessor to the beanie and rather natty in grey and blue – which we pulled down to cover our ears until the first light of day, at which point the imperative not to look a total and certifiable nerd took precedence over the alternative of freezing half to death.

My bike was locked in a sort of cupboard outside, which was one of a terraced row of sheds designed for people to be able to lock up their prams, and which linked two of the blocks of flats. The handlebars of my bike were always entangled with those of my brother's, and also with our homemade go-kart, which was made out of a disused pram, an orange box and an old door. Crammed into this little cupboard we also kept stuff like our wellies, suitcases, a bit of accumulated camping gear, including an assortment of hurricane lamps, and an old budgerigar cage. Anything, in fact, which could not easily be stored in the flat.

After an awkward five minutes trying to extract the bike from everything else, without waking up the neighbours or causing too much damage to all the rest of this clutter, I'd eventually get my shit together and cycle a mile to the paper shop. There was usually an icy wind blasting into my face, which lent to my ears a colour and luminosity which would be an effective warning to low-flying aircraft. By the time I arrived I was often soaked to the skin and practically stiff with cold.

Any of this ring a bell with you?

Once there, a miserable old scrote with a deeply suspect teddy-boy haircut and a cigarette hanging out of his mouth would jerk a nicotine-stained finger towards a pile of newspapers about a foot high. Somehow or other I would have to try to manhandle this wedge of papers into what seemed to be a huge canvas bag with 'Evening News' written in block black letters on the side. I was so short in those days that I'd have to tie a knot in the

strap to prevent this bag from trailing around my ankles as I hob-
bled out of the shop, bent over sideways by the weight. Even now
I can feel the strap digging into my shoulders.

At that age – maybe about nine I reckon – I could hardly
bloody lift the bag, let alone ride my bike with it strapped over
my shoulder. So in an early example of what turned out to be the
enterprise that stood us both in good stead later in life, my
brother and I managed to envisage and draw a design for an
ingenious metal device which would enable us to carry these
unwieldy bags across our handlebars. I'm not sure now who
made them for us, but someone did, and so these metal frame-
works became permanent fixtures on the front forks of our bikes.

This new technique of carrying half a hundredweight of newspapers had the desirable effect of preventing the strap from digging painfully into the shoulder and cutting off the circulation of
blood to our heads and arms. On the other hand it also made the
bicycle alarmingly unstable and top-heavy, so that at any
moment we were in danger of toppling over into the path of an
oncoming car – not that there were all that many cars around in
1960, and even fewer on the streets at six in the morning.

I do remember trying to park the bike against the kerb while I
went in to a block of flats to deliver half a dozen papers, only to
find when I returned that a gust of wind had blown it over, and
all the newspapers were strewn across the road, covered in mud
and accumulating rainwater. Oh joy of joys. The memory of trying to collect up the papers, page by page, attempting to re-
assemble them into the correct editions, and then trying to put
them back in the intended order of delivery – all with freezing
cold fingers and in a howling gale – still rather traumatises me
when I think about it some forty-five years later. Are you getting
all this? Great intro to the world of work, huh?

I guess that it was about this time that I started hating readers of the *Daily Telegraph*. Not that I had anything against their

politics or even the fact that most of them lived in what seemed to me to be impossibly grand houses with long garden paths. At the age of nine I hadn't put any of these ingredients together. No, my objection to *Daily Telegraph* readers was that they ordered a big newspaper, but had a small letter box. I'm not sure why my venom on this subject seems to revolve around the *Daily Telegraph*; I'm fairly sure that *The Times* and the *Financial Times* were of equal proportions, but for some reason it does. Even in those days – pre-colour supplements, or indeed pre every other idiotic addition from property to finance, from motoring to sport, from gardening to 'living' – even then the *Telegraph* was a big fat newspaper, and wouldn't go through the average letter box without being divided into sections.

If you haven't ever had a paper-round, you have almost certainly never given this a thought. If you have, you know exactly what I am talking about. Every letter box has its own particular characteristics – some are hard to push open and you can dislocate your thumb in the attempt; others have a tendency to slam closed so hard and fast that you are in daily danger of losing a digit. Still others have a ferocious dog on the other side which takes a savage bite at any protuberance which pokes through the door, and which makes no concessions whatever to tiny childish fingers. It gives a whole new perspective to biting ones nails. Some letter boxes are too high and on the vertical, others are too low and on the horizontal, while still others have a box or a cage behind them so that a newspaper won't go sufficiently far in to be sure that it won't topple out. And almost all of them are too small, especially for a broadsheet newspaper.

So that instead of being able to walk down the path, push the paper through the letter box with a single action and be on your way, you'd have to get to the door, put down everything else you were carrying onto the wet doormat, divide up the newspaper into manageable sections, and slot them through one after

another. Oh how I used to envy those little bastards in the
American TV shows whose bicycles had those fantastic cow-horn
handlebars that we all coveted, and who would not even hesitate
in their pedalling as they hurled their newspapers up a long
drive. Life was not much like that for us.

Sitting there in your warm and comfortable armchair or whatever you are doing while reading this now, I'm sure that all this
doesn't seem like much of a hardship. But transport yourself back
to the mind of an over-tired, freezing cold and wet nine-year-old,
and you can probably understand why one of many early promises made to self in those days was to ensure that any letter box
in any front door of any house that I might eventually have cus-
tody of would be big enough to accommodate whatever newspaper I ordered in a single sweep. Just like a promise I made to
myself years later while hitchhiking in the driving rain that I
would always stop for a hitchhiker if I had a spare seat in my car.
Have I kept to either of these promises? Have I bollocks. Of
course not. A worrying proportion of hitchhikers turned out to be
psychopathic murderers, and newspapers are three times the
dimensions they were in those days. Meanwhile letter boxes are
– well, they're letter boxes.

And all this for ten bob a week. Yep, that's right. 50p in deci-
mal. I think it went up to 11/6d after I'd done it for a year or so.

That said, I think that I'm probably lucky that in my life there
are only about half a dozen things about which I quite literally
cringe with embarrassment when I recall them and there is an
aspect to this, which I'm afraid gives rise to one of them. To the
extent that it's been in and out of this draft half a dozen times and
in the end I've just said 'do you know what, let's see if we can get
it out in the open and get over it'. So here it is.

In the few days coming up to Christmas, I went around the
route of my paper-round, knocking on every door, and when it
was answered I was standing there on the doorstep saying

'Christmas tip for the paper-boy?' All joking to one side, I've seen a fair bit of shit in my life, but as I sit here at 6.08 on a Sunday morning writing this, I feel a heavy weight in my chest, and my blood pressure rising.

The passing years and a natural instinct for survival has expunged the details of any responses, and I suspect that the vast majority of the householders just thought me a pushy little oik from the wrong side of the tracks, but nonetheless went back into the house and returned with two bob, or whatever. I seem to think that at the end of this exercise, I had accumulated maybe about £5, which was an absolute bloody fortune, and hard-earned in just about every sense of the words.

What can I have been thinking? And how did the little boy who was prepared to do that without it occurring to me that this was embarrassing, turn into the old git who is so totally morti-fied by it now? Anyway, it's out there; make of it what you will. Even in those early days, I was a little twot.

The milk-round

So yes, the early introduction to the world of work wasn't too aus-picious, and in addition to the paper-round, both my brother and I also used to help the milkman on a Saturday, which was our one day off from delivering newspapers. On Saturdays, instead of getting up at 5.30, we would get up at 4.30 and cycle a mile and a half to the milk depot. My brother used to help a very nice bloke called Cyril – not a name you hear much these days – and I used to help a very nice bloke called Tom, which nowadays seems to be the name given to one in every three boys in any junior school. Amazing huh? Wouldn't it be something if it was the other way around? A lot of bloody Cyrils.

Cyril had a regular round so that after a while my brother got to know the houses and what they ordered. Two silver tops and one gold. A pint of gold top and a pint of 'stera' – remember that?

It was in an elegant little bottle with a prise-off top. Whatever happened to the appetite for sterilised milk, do you suppose?

Once again, in my memory it was always cold, and so there was a constant danger that my numb little fingers would slip off the top of a wet and shiny bottle of milk, leaving shattered glass and huge puddles all over the step.

Unlike Cyril, Tom was a sort of inspector character who used to have to do a different round every week, probably to ensure that his colleagues weren't embezzling the gold off of the gold tops or something, but that meant that I never had the chance to familiarise myself with an individual milk-round. And equally, therefore, never got the chance to ingratiate myself with mothers in well-to-do neighbourhoods who would take pity on a poor brat from the local estate and hand over a warm cup of Bovril and a slice of toast and dripping.

Tom, on the other hand, seemed to enjoy benefits-in-kind from a whole lot of different women, but this isn't that sort of book, so probably best to forget that I mentioned it. All I cared about was that the odd fifteen-minute delay here and there held us up, so that the round that should have been finished by lunchtime took until about 2 p.m., by which time I was ready for the plate full of grease and cholesterol to which he treated me in the café before giving me my 12/6p.

Not bad eh? I could earn slightly more for one morning's work than for getting up early the other six days. Taken together, I was making more than £1 a week which was, I may tell you, living.

The newsagent

The obligations of school and the limitations of age meant that these were the only jobs it was possible for me to have until the age of about fourteen, by which time my family had moved a little way up-market and further out in the 'burbs to Elmers End, where I was able to get a Saturday job in the local newsagent. I can't remember much about it except that, of course, at that age I was consumingly preoccupied with everything to do with girls, and so the best thing about the job was that it provided an occasional chance to have a conversation with that most mysterious of species.

The job also provided an even more occasional opportunity to leaf briefly and furtively through the inside pages of risqué magazines which in no circumstances whatsoever could one have actually bought. However, as risqué as they got in the newsagent at Elmers End was probably *Tit-Bits* which, I'm sorry to say, failed the Ronseal test, and did not do what it said on the label.

Everyone smoked cigarettes in those days, so most orders included a request for '20 number 6', or '20 Players'. You could tell a toff because he smoked Benson and Hedges, and you could tell a hard man because he smoked Capstan Full Strength. Women and woolly woofters smoked Peter Stuyvesant or some other menthol brand, hippies smoked roll-ups and beatniks smoked Gauloise. (If you're too young to know what a beatnik is, you probably shouldn't be reading this book.) All that was before you got to the cigars and the pipe tobacco.

This job was sort of OK, but it was only busy in the mornings and they didn't need me after lunch, so when the opportunity arose to get a full day of work in with the greengrocer up the road, I jumped at it.

The greengrocer

The job in the greengrocer's also involved very early starts, but it was there that I learned all the valuable things about fruit and vegetables that a young city boy had never had the opportunity to find out about hitherto. Most of my experience of vegetables until then had involved a tin and a tin-opener. I'm not sure that I even knew that vegetables grew in the ground. However, I was a quick learner, and before you could say 'aubergine' I knew the difference between a cos and a webb's wonder, what is an 'ugli', and that beetroots have to be cooked; and that's to take but three examples from a choice of several dozen. More revelatory still, was the much-more-useful discovery that suburban housewives will put up with an absolutely breathtaking amount of suggestive flirting from anyone with the brass neck to try it on.

This greengrocer's shop on Elmers End High Street was run by two blokes called Jeff and John. Jeff was a very nice, very gentle Greek bloke, who was actually the owner of the shop and whose sister lived upstairs. However Jeff's sister co-habited with John, who was without doubt the lowest form of human life I had come across at that stage, and that was quite a claim.

John was an original white-van-man long before the term had been invented. At fourteen I guess I must have been something of a late developer because these were still very much formative years for me, and John's obsession with sex left me awe-struck. He was about twenty-five and his preoccupation made mine seem positively part-time. We're all now familiar with the decades of puerile comedy which have been derived from the phallic nature of various salad and vegetable items, but the early sight of John trying to ram a cucumber into a women's shopping bag, held at around about waist height, and yelling 'I can't get it all in' was an early and fairly vivid introduction.

John was nothing if not imaginative and exhaustive in his quest to find innuendo in anything and everything. He never missed an opportunity to point out a nodule on a potato which could remind the tortured mind of a nipple. He could never sell anyone a melon without picking up two and holding them against his chest to give the customer a choice. He'd offer every-one in the shop the chance to take a little squeeze of one, and then a little squeeze of the other, and he would whoop, appar-ently hilariously, as though the pressure points were personal. No, there was practically no end to his inventiveness. Courgettes, carrots and parsnips all had their roles in his repertoire of suggestiveness. Soft fruit in general and figs in particular had all the connotations I later learned more about from the pen of D.H. Lawrence. A combination of tomatoes and a cucumber could provide hours of harmless jollity. But most amazing of all, to me at least, was that all the women appeared to love it.

It's not like he was Dean Martin or Frankie Vaughan or whomever else women fancied at the time – this bloke was a squat little git who looked as though he could do with a good wash. However, this continual tirade of – I was going to say double-entendres but actually these were singularly singular entendres – seemed to draw them in like magnets. Also, it wasn't as though there was no choice – these were days well before the Tesco Metro, or indeed any other supermarket – but there was another perfectly decent greengrocer in the same row of shops. While that shop remained as quiet as the local library, at our end of the street there was a constant queue of women. Good old Jeff used to think that this was because our produce was of higher quality or value, but John and I knew better.

What did all this teach me? Nothing that I was ever able to find useful because, however much I might have wished to be able to open up the subject of sex with girls or women, I would have been no more capable of approaching the matter in the way that John did than I would of joining the Beverley Sisters. However, I do remember on one occasion that I was on the receiving end of a very overt proposition from a married woman of about 30 to deliver her purchases to her house after work. I recall torturing myself all day long with the prospect, before mentioning it to Jeff, who counselled against. Now buoyed up with bravado, I asked him what the problem was.

'Ask yourself this,' he said, with a wisdom which belied his appearance, 'do you want to put yourself in a position where another bloke could come around and carve off your balls with a

rusty knife, and you would know that he was entirely justified?'
A vivid thought, I imagine you'll agree, and so in these early
impressionable years my terror overcame my lust, and my own
particular Mrs Robinson had to find her graduate somewhere
else.

Anyway, one day Jeff came to work on a Saturday and told me
that John had vanished. Just upped and left in the night. We
never did know what happened to him. Maybe an irate husband
chopped him up and buried him in a suburban garden. It would
have been less than he deserved.

So much for my salad days.

The restaurant

Those were some of the jobs my brother and I used to have during ordinary term-time, but of course the summer holidays provided opportunities for full-time working, and several of these
yielded lessons which we may find interesting and worthwhile as
we begin to understand the overall perspective on the world of
work as viewed by a Grumpy.

For example, at one time during a school summer holiday I got
a job for a few weeks as a kitchen helper and waiter in the
restaurant of what was then Nicholson's Department Store in
Bromley High Street. It was there that I learned a very valuable
lesson about the thing called 'looking busy', which was to stand
me in good stead in quite a few jobs in later life.

Nicholson's was a busy store and this was a busy restaurant,
and there were only about half a dozen of us running the entire
operation. My basic job was to do the washing-up, and this was
pre-dishwashers so I spent most of the day with my hands in
sinks full of scalding hot water. In between washing dishes I used
to do a bit of waiting on some tables, which provided another
opportunity to meet and talk to girls, albeit in circumstances
which I found faintly humiliating.

The memorable thing about this job was that one or two of the other people working in the kitchen had what I suppose these days we would call 'learning difficulties'. What we called them at the time does not pass the modern PC test, so I'll leave it to your imagination. However, I do remember that at various times of the day one of these good women would stop whatever it was she was doing, grab a cloth, and start rubbing a surface with unnatural vigour and tell the rest of us to 'look busy'. Being of a slightly sharper persuasion myself, it took me only a little while to work out that these incidents were occasioned by the arrival in the kitchen of anyone who might be described as 'management'. This category seemed to include just about anyone else on the whole staff of the department store, because everyone was senior to the half a dozen of us who worked in the kitchens. We were the lowest of the low.

Rubbing down a work-surface with a damp cloth is no doubt a plausible way of 'looking busy', but actually there was a severe limit to other ways to 'look busy' in a confined space. One could reach for a broom and commence sweeping an already spotless floor, or one could reach for a mop and start mopping some tiles which had recently been mopped. But these were the days before computers which can, at the press of a button, flick your screen from booking your hols on lastminute.com or some vile pornography, to a screen showing a spreadsheet. And so I quickly ran out of alternatives for 'looking busy' and was happy to allow others to do my share of 'looking busy' for me.

This in its own way is sad enough, but the saddest thing of all is that we all worked like Peruvian silver miners. At about 2/6p an hour, this was as close to slave labour as you're going to get in the western world, and the work was exhausting and more or less relentless. The idea that, if someone else on the staff happened to come in at one of the very few moments when you were not legitimately working up a sweat, you had to appear to be working up a sweat, seemed to me in those young idealistic times to be unacceptable. To the extent that I believe I said something to the effect of 'blow that for a game of soldiers' and continued to do whatever it was I had or had not been doing.

This led to consternation among my colleagues, who were certain that I was courting disaster. I was of course fortunate that their idea of disaster wasn't the same as my idea of disaster, but nonetheless it's grim to think of these poor bloody oompah loompahs being afraid of any jumped-up toss-pot in a suit who looked and sounded like an authority figure.

The other very useful thing I learned in the restaurant was of course one of the ten golden rules of life, which is never to be rude to anyone who is involved with preparing or serving your food. For the sake of your entertainment I could of course make up stories about my former colleagues gobbing into the soup destined for one of the many irritating or supercilious douche-bags who thought it was OK to be demanding or overbearing with people they made the mistake of treating as their inferiors. Truth to tell I never actually witnessed this precise remedy. Perhaps it would just suffice to say that standards of hygiene were not the highest priority when dealing with such people, and that a mouse-dropping can look very like a sultana when inserted by pressure of a grubby thumb into the side of a fruited scone.

Needless to say, the job at Nicholson's didn't last long because one day four people my own age came in – two blokes and two girls – and one of the boys decided that it would be a good idea to impress his girlfriend by treating me like a servant. It's amazing how hot a bowl of soup can be when deposited onto the lap of a pair of Levis, and equally amazing how quickly one can find oneself out of work after such an incident. I think I was probably on the street even before he reached the casualty department – and with not even a tip to show for it.

The library

Obviously all this was well before 'gap years' as we know them now, but unlike most of my mates who went straight from school to university I did in fact take a gap year. But instead of travelling around Vietnam or backpacking across Australia as they do today, I got to spend quite a lot of time in Lewisham.

For example, I worked for a while in Lewisham Library as a library assistant, and boy oh boy what a total bore that was. I was planning to study English at university, and think I must have reckoned that working in a library would be cool because that would give me the chance to read a lot of books. Did it? Did it bog-roll. What it gave me the chance to do was to strengthen my upper arms under the weight of huge piles of books published by Mills and Boon, which women would simply take off the shelves in multiples of eight a week, without even looking to see if they had read them before.

It didn't matter if they had read them or not. All of them had the same story, in which Lord Drogo would fall in love, despite himself and to the disapproval of his family, with a humble servant girl or other assorted wench, and would sweep her off her feet. These were early days in my chosen hobby of amateur psychologist, but even I could work out that their insatiable enthusiasm for this old tosh said something significant about the lives of our typical readers. I think we called these 'romances' at the time and it was only later that I learned that they are better known as 'bodice-rippers'. Not that there were a lot of bodices about among the ladies of Lewisham in 1969.

While I did not get the smallest chance to do any actual reading, I did learn something which has proven useful to know for the rest of my life since and which, who knows, may be of use to you. Especially if for some reason only you could explain you are considering a career working in a library. What I learned in the library was a whole new level of vindictiveness and pettiness which had been outside of my experience hitherto.

I don't suppose you've ever given this a thought – why would you – but there are, in your local library, two levels of staff. One is the 'professional librarian' who has been to Library School or studied librarianship at some further education college or whatever, and the other is the lowly 'library assistants' whom they more or less recruit off the street. Being local authority workers, all of these people have very rigid levels of rank and seniority based on qualifications and time served, each level bringing a new pay scale, extra benefits and holidays etc.

However, the real difference between these two is that the junior lot are a regular group of people just doing a fairly menial job for not a lot of money, and the senior lot are a bunch of arseholes. If you are not a proven Grumpy yourself, you're obviously thinking that this is too sweeping a generalisation, and usually I'd agree, but on this occasion I'm afraid it's a close-to-universal truth. All professional librarians, with the single exception of my friend Tina, are arseholes.

The root of all this is, of course, that librarianship is a very boring job which a complete know-nothing could learn everything there is to know about in approximately twenty-seven minutes. However, because of the very rigid pay structure and seniority, and the very flimsy nature of their claim to any professional status, qualified librarians have to take every possible opportunity to emphasise anything which distinguishes them from their junior assistants.

So that, if a reader would come to the desk where I was checking books in and out, all I was allowed to do was to check the books in and out. If this reader had any questions to ask – any questions at all – I would be obliged to refer them to the Enquiry Desk, at which sat one of the qualified and professional librarians. He or she would usually be preoccupied with working out his or her days off for the next calendar year, so that they could be fitted to optimal advantage around bank holidays. Such was the tyrannical nature of the hierarchy that all of the professionals' leave-days had to be booked and settled before any of the juniors could book even a day off to get married. Elderly parents were obliged to die at the weekends so that the junior could be back at work on the Monday.

Often, however, there would be a queue of people waiting to be dealt with at the Enquiry Desk, and the particular reader's enquiry would be an entirely simple matter. But still I, as a junior and not professionally qualified library assistant, was not allowed to answer it.

'Where', for example, 'were the car manuals?' A relatively difficult one this, and one that you would have to have worked in the library for at least an hour or so to be able to answer, but having tidied the books every day for a week I knew their Dewey number and which shelf they were on as well as I knew the price

of a pint of draft Guinness in the Jolly Farmers public house next door. Was I allowed to answer the question? No I was not. I had to refer the enquirer to the Enquiry Desk where they had to queue to get their answer.

In Lewisham Library at that time, all of the non-fiction books were stacked on shelves in the middle of the main hall, and all of the fiction books were stacked A–L, M–Z on the opposing walls at each end. As a junior library assistant one was not allowed, on fear of noisy reprimand, to point this out to anyone who asked where the fiction was.

Day in day out I would get into trouble with one or other of these toss-pot librarians for answering the most elementary question rather than referring members of the rate-paying public to the end of a queue. And the ire of these plonkers was heightened by the fact that they knew I had no plans to make working in the library system my career, and so was not terrified of the disciplinary procedure.

Finally, and I promise that this is true, a bloke with failing eyesight came to the check-in desk where I was serving and asked me what the time was. There was a big clock on the wall and he couldn't see it. When I told him that I was sorry but that I wasn't allowed to deal with enquiries from members of the public, and that he'd have to ask at the Enquiry Desk, the shit hit the fan. Obviously I thought I was being funny. Plainly, had I for some reason been so tired of having an actual life that I had wished to pursue that of a librarian, this was not going to happen.

The craven nature of the hierarchical system, and the advantage taken of this by the most senior ranks of the library service, also meant that everyone who worked in the library lived in continuing dread of upsetting a member of the public. If you were the subject of a complaint from a ratepayer, no matter how unjustified that complaint, or how excellent the service you had actually given, there would be a black mark against your record. A cloud hanging over your prospects of advancement. You might not get your next increment, or your excrement, or whatever.

As a librarian in the London Borough of Lewisham, you were never going to be given the benefit of the doubt. The readers were always going to be in the right, and you were always going to be in the wrong. If it was their word against yours, your word wasn't worth shit.

As a result, the average librarian in the Borough of Lewisham would go to inordinate lengths to avoid offending or upsetting a member of the reading public, no matter how unreasonable or objectionable they were being.

Anyone who has tried to provide a service for the public, or who has dealt with the public on a regular basis, knows just how utterly appalling they can be. Personally I was stunned that ordinary people could be such awful and unreasonable arse-heads. There seemed to be no end to the number of rude, impatient, imperious loud-mouths who thought it was OK to be gratuitously offensive to the staff in the library, just because they were being paid out of their rates.

In the whole borough, however, there was just one member of the library staff – just one bloke – to whom none of this applied. For though in his ordinary appearance Mr Ericsson seemed to be an average run-of-the-mill branch librarian, Mr Ericsson had a secret which marked him out from his colleagues. A secret which gave him a charmed life and made it seem to us like maybe he was an eccentric millionaire who had come to work in the library service just to see how the other half lives.

Yes. Mr Ericsson was a friend of the Town Clerk, and being a friend of the Town Clerk made Mr Ericsson as close to invulnerable as it was possible to be and still remain an earthling. What was more, Mr Ericsson played golf with the Town Clerk every Wednesday afternoon, and this meant that no-one else in the library service, even his superiors, was allowed to enquire why he was not at his post on those days. Mr Ericsson had a 'get out of jail free' card hidden away in his pocket, and as good fortune would have it, he and I happened to be working together one afternoon in an outlying branch when he got the opportunity to play it.

It was a Tuesday afternoon in November, I believe, and I was on the check-in desk doing a bit of quiet filing, when a very smart-looking woman with a very ferocious expression on her face strode in and slammed down a postcard on the counter.

'I want to speak to the person who sent me this,' she said. This was not one of our Mills & Boon readers. Plainly we were much more in Miss Marple territory, and this was a character from the big house.

I looked at the card and could see that it was one of our routine reminders indicating that the reader had a book out that was overdue. All of these cards were posted out with a generic signature of the branch librarian, but obviously I was the man on the spot, and so I was about to take the wrap. However, just over my shoulder I could sense Mr Ericsson stepping forward, and he more or less elbowed me to one side.

'I did,' he said. 'What seems to be the trouble?' His tone betrayed no sense that he was intimidated by her stroppy manner, and this had the effect of irritating her more.

'I have received this card through the post, and it says that I have taken this book from the library and failed to return it.' Her horse was getting higher by the second. 'I am here to inform you that I have never borrowed this book, and therefore that I have no intention of returning it.'

Ericsson didn't speak, but picked up the reminder and walked over to the card index, where we kept the readers' tickets. Do you remember those? There was a little brown cardboard pocket with your name and address written on it, into which would be inserted a little brown cardboard slip bearing the name of the book and the author. You've probably got one hidden away inside the cover of a book which has been on a forgotten shelf these last thirty years, languishing as the overdue fine spirals into six figures.

You can say what you like about old technology, but the great virtue of the brown ticket system was that you had the tangible evidence right there in your hand. Ericsson fiddled about in the file for a few moments and returned to the counter. He held up a brown library card and a brown book-ticket and said:

'Is this your library ticket?'

The woman agreed that it was.

'And is this the ticket for the book mentioned on the reminder?'

She looked at it closely and agreed that it was.

'Then you have the book, and it is overdue for return, which is why I sent you the reminder.'

At this, the women looked fit to explode, and any librarian in the borough who was a mere mortal would have shrunk under the ferocity of her gaze, shuddering at the likelihood of upsetting her further. Cringing at the prospect that she would complain to a higher being. But this was not just any run of the mill librarian. This was Mr Ericsson, and Mr Ericsson was a close personal friend of the Town Clerk. They played golf together on a Wednesday afternoon.

'I have told you already that I do not have this book.'

'Yes you do,' he said. 'Here is your ticket, and here is the ticket that has come out of the book.'

'I do not,' she said

'Yes you do,' he replied.

'I do not.'

'You do.'

With that, the woman wheeled around like a dervish and strode towards the door. She was nearly at the exit when suddenly she stopped, paused, seemed to think of something, and then turned around and marched back towards the counter.

'Just before I go directly to the Town Hall to complain about you,' she said, 'let me see if I have got this right.'

I wasn't sure what was coming next. The situation seemed to be so very simple. What could there be that needed further clarification? Finally she raised herself up still further, and the words when they came out were like carvings on his tombstone.

'Are you', she said with as much menace as a suburban housewife could possibly muster, 'calling me a liar?'

By this time, I have to say, Mr Ericsson had already assumed the level of super-hero in my book for having stood up to her so robustly, so I would have been ready to understand and forgive him if he had chosen this moment to reduce the temperature just a bit. Anyone might have. He'd made his point. He didn't have to continue to pursue it. He could retreat just slightly. But did he? Did he hell. I don't think he even paused to consider his next response, and I remember it word for word as if this happened yesterday.

'Yes,' he said, leaving no room for doubt, 'you are a liar. And not only that, but you are also a stinking liar, and I want that book back in my branch by 5 o'clock tonight.'

Well, if he had been lighter and I had been either stronger or gay, I would have raised him on my shoulders and carried him out of the building. It was a moment to savour. The woman looked so swollen with indignation that at any moment her epidermis would peel off and be left on the floor like an overripe banana skin. Evidently she was too angry to speak, so she said nothing more and walked out.

Old Ericsson didn't say anything very much for the rest of the afternoon, and I didn't say anything very much either. However, I watched the clock as it ticked around towards closing time and, believe it or not, at ten minutes to five the women appeared back at the door of the library, accompanied by a lad of about fourteen who was looking very very sheepish and was carrying a book under his arm.

She took the book from him and placed it on the counter. 'I am sorry,' she said, 'it seems that my son took out the book using my ticket without my knowledge. I really didn't know anything about it.'

Ericsson took the book, took the postcard, and consulted a table on the counter in front of us.

'That'll be 1/9d,' said Ericsson (yes that's right – decimalisation was still two years away), and he took her money and allowed it to drop with a pleasing clatter into the fines box. What a day!

So that was the library, but before we pass on, I must just quickly tell you the story of John, who was one of the drivers whose job it was to transport crate-loads of books from one branch to another. John drove a Land Rover, and among his many duties was to tow a bloody big caravan containing the mobile library to each of the four corners of the borough. Once he had arrived, he would uncouple the trailer and leave the mobile library there for the afternoon, being very careful to put a padlock on the handbrake, because it was not unknown for the local heroes to release the brake so that the mobile library and all its books and occupants risked a spectacular slalom down the hill. Once secured in place, the local women would come in and swap the eight romances they had just read for another eight romances they had read just a few weeks ago. Manning the mobile library for several afternoons a week was one of my responsibilities, of which more in a moment.

Anyway, John the driver was an absolutely excellent bloke of about 55, who had once had a very senior job in the construction business, but had on some occasion suffered a terrible accident and sustained a serious blow to the head. This had caused an alarming hole on one side of his forehead which made him look as though he could lie on his back and provide a very suitable substitute for an egg-cup. However, rather more seriously, it had left him with a total loss of his short-term memory. John was a highly entertaining and highly intelligent bloke who could remember the arithmetical formula which enabled you to decide how many bricks it would take to build the Royal Albert Hall, but who could not remember what he did an hour earlier.

Now I've found throughout my life that you can always tell a low-grade manager by the way he treats the people working for him and, in particular, you can always tell a low-grade manager who is also an arsehole by the way he bullies anyone he thinks he can get away with bullying. In this case the branch manager, a Mr Earnshaw, fell neatly and squarely into the second of these two categories, and so felt able to treat poor old John with a sort of contempt which, had John been in his pre-accident condition, would have left the bastard sitting on the pavement spitting out blood and teeth.

However, life isn't fair, the accident had happened, and now John was reduced to having to be treated like a half-wit by numb-skulls, even though he had twice the brainpower of any three of the rest of us.

John managed his memory-loss for the most part with a great sense of humour, and with the use of plenty of maps which would enable him to look up the routes to and from the various library branches around the borough on a daily basis. All this was usu-ally fine. It was not always quite so fine, however, when John had towed the mobile library out into one of the far-flung housing estates where it and I would sit for several hours in the after-noon. The reason was that John would quite frequently forget where he had left me, or indeed that he had left me anywhere at all.

Usually he would tow me out at about lunchtime, and then come and pick me up about 5 p.m. so that I could get back to the library for six. Quite often, though, 5 p.m. would come and go, the evening was beginning to draw in, and there was no sign of John or his trusty Land Rover. Even this wouldn't have been too bad, but for the fact that one or two of these estates were fairly close to what we would now call bandit country, and once or twice the level of stones, bottles and assorted debris which rained down on the roof of the caravan made it feel a bit like defending the Alamo.

John and I were mates, and so the last thing I wanted to do was to lock up the mobile library, go in search of a phone box (these were the days before the mobile phone) and call the main branch to find out where he was. This would be likely to get him into even more trouble, and in the way of some further humiliation or bullying from the vile Mr Earnshaw.

Usually on these occasions John would eventually consult his daily duty roster and discover that he had to collect me, or one of my other mates would remind him, and he would trace on the map the route to whichever far-flung and god-forsaken out-post of the borough he had left me. Usually he would arrive just ahead of the arsonists.

John's best feature was his sense of humour, and this was what sustained him through the tribulations of being treated like a half-wit by people who should have known better. In fact he managed to see the funny side right up to this particular day when the branch librarian Mr Earnshaw waved him over in his habitual imperious manner and with even more than his usual level of patronising contempt, said something like:

'I say John old boy, I wonder if you would be a good fellow and cast your mind back to that book I asked you to bring from Deptford last night?' Earnshaw looked over the top of his glasses rather as one might look at an errant schoolboy in a prep-school. 'I need it for a reader who has requested it and I was wondering, John old bean, what the bloody hell you have done with it?'

You hear a lot about the last straw that broke the camel's back, but I've found in life that you are seldom close enough to hear the snap. On this occasion I did. John didn't hesitate for a second, and the look in his eyes left no doubt that this was going to be a defining moment in his life. 'Mr Earnshaw,' he said, beautifully calm, and with no trace of anger or rancour in his tone, 'I can't remember what I had for breakfast, and if I could, do you think I'd be working in this crap-hole, for an irritating piece of shit like you?'

With that, John got his hat and went off to what I hope proved to be a long and happy retirement. I never got the chance to ask him; not that he would have been able to remember if it was happy or not.

The hospice

By now I was about nineteen, and somehow or other I got a job as a porter at a hospice. At the time I didn't even know what a hospice was, but then again nor did very many other people because I believe they had only recently been invented in this country. Or maybe they had been re-invented because their predecessors had been very much of the very grim 'abandon hope all ye who enter' variety.

The idea of a cheerful and sunny place to which you could go after all remedial treatment has failed and where your pain and suffering can be managed so that your passing can be peaceful, was all very new then, and the term hospice was not in common usage. Nonetheless, I was not so stupid that I hadn't worked out what it was when I went for the job.

The selection procedure was cursory. Though by this time I was looking like a weirdo of the hippy variety, I didn't look too much like a weirdo of the necrophiliac variety, and also I didn't look as though I had a sideline of the Burke and Hare kind. I would do. My responsibilities were all the ones you might expect of a hospital porter, with the difference that it was never easy to get out of one's head the thought that just about everybody I had to deal with in an average day was shortly going to die.

This isn't the place to go into all that – we're grumpy enough as it is. However, amazingly, even this did have its lighter moments. One involved my responsibility of going around the wards every morning selling newspapers. The wards had three or four people in each, in various states of malaise, and there was one bloke called Mr Potter who had not spoken to anyone for the whole six weeks that he had been there. No-one knew whether the problem was that he could not speak, or that he could speak but didn't want to. He was just not communicating at all other than through very occasional and barely perceptible nods of the head.

I think that someone must have told me when I took over the job that Mr Potter liked to get the *Daily Mail*, and so I would leave the paper for him, and pick up coins to the value of the purchase price which he always left on his bedside table. Usually I'd stop and chat for a minute or two, telling him what the weather was like and so on; never expecting a response and never getting one.

I think I did this for about two or three weeks when a day came that he didn't have any small change on his side table, or I didn't have any small change in my pocket, and so I told him that I would owe him 10 pence which I reassured him that I would pay on my round tomorrow.

Next day came, I did my rounds selling the papers, and when I got to Mr Potter's bed, he seemed to be asleep. So I left his newspaper on the edge of the bed and took some change from a little pile of coins on the bedside table. I was on my way to the next ward when suddenly I heard an unfamiliar voice from behind me.

'Stuart'. I was amazed, and the nurses were amazed, and the doctors were amazed, and all of us amazed people hurried back to Mr Potter's bedside, wondering if we were about to have the privilege of hearing his dying words. Being the nearest person at hand, when I got there I put my head close to his lips so that I wouldn't miss a syllable. I strained to hear.

I saw his lips quiver as they tried to form the words which were evidently creating such a burden in his brain that he had to break his long silence to get them out. Eventually he did.

'You owe me ten pence,' he said. He then didn't speak another word before he died, just about a week later.

So much for famous last words huh? That was one for the history books.

A Proper Job

I remember when I was a kid, and our family would be in the car on the way to the shops or wherever, one of my mother's constant themes was how workmen were always leaning on their shovels. 'Look at them,' she'd say, usually as we were being held up by some roadworks, 'that bloke has been standing there talking to his mate the whole time we've been waiting.' Then she would complain about the bone-idle British workman and suggest that this was the reason 'the country is going to the dogs'.

'The country going to the dogs' was one of many contemporary expressions used in my family, the meaning of which I had no idea about. Obviously I knew what dogs were; even at that age I knew they were nasty smelly things which shat profusely all over pavements and our football pitch. But that didn't give me much of a clue as to what 'the dogs' were in this context, nor did I have any point of comparison which would indicate whether we were going to them or not. However, at that age you tend to take what your parents say as gospel, so I must have assumed that 'the dogs' was not a place to which we collectively wanted to go, and that if we were indeed en route to them, it was largely the fault of that bloke leaning on this shovel.

That was my assumption, at least, until one day I got a job involving a shovel.

How did I get such a job? Whatever talents I may or may not have possessed from a decent education gained entirely at the expense of the state, knowing how to operate a shovel certainly wasn't among them. No, I got that job in the same way that you probably got your job – though bullshit – a subject which merits another brief diversion before we revert to the matter of manual labour.

Quite frequently these days I find myself involved in conversations involving friends or colleagues where one of them is talking about a younger person and complaining that they are 'full of bullshit'. Though I love to engage in a communal gripe as much as the next Grump, there is something about this particular allegation that makes me hesitate before joining in the chorus. And that's because I've found that bullshit has served me very well over the years.

By now I was at university. Hair halfway down to my arse, scruffy sideburns and wispy beard, darts cut off from purple corduroy sewn into the seams of my Levis to make them even more flared, a floral scarf tied around my knee or my head, and a Second World War trench-coat. What a bloody state.

Having worked for a year after school, I left home aged nineteen to go to Newcastle University and, being that it was a long way away and being that I was a self-centred and inconsiderate little sod, it was another year before I came home. In that time I hadn't shaved or had a haircut, and had lost a stone and a half in weight. When finally I returned to my family home in Beckenham I knocked on the door, my mother answered, took one look at me and burst into tears. This was one of the early occasions when I should have been grateful for this country's strict laws on the control of firearms. Had we lived in Alabama she would almost certainly have shot me, and the judge would have declared it to be a justifiable homicide. Anyway the reason I was back was not because of home-sickness or consideration for my long-suffering parents. It was because I had no money to pay my rent through the holidays in Newcastle and needed to doss with them and get a job. Maybe I could have gone back to the mortuary or the library, but that didn't seem cool enough for me. For some reason it seemed much cooler at the time to be doing something manual, and so I borrowed my mother's Morris 1000 and drove around looking for a building site.

The first one I came to was in Bromley. Half a dozen houses were half-built up to the level of the first floor, and there were three blokes working flat out running up and down ladders. I approached the guy who looked like the boss and asked if he had any work for a manual labourer.

Can you imagine the way this bloke looked at me? He was quite a short bloke, but built like the proverbial brick-shithouse. He was a rough, tough, sinewy bundle of muscle, and in comparison I was a blancmange. Sure I was tall and sure I was thin, but in comparison to these blokes I was like Bonnie Langford to his Lennox Lewis. With about the same chance of prevailing in any physical dispute.

He asked if I had experience as a builder's labourer and, of course, I said yes I had, I could do it with my eyes closed. What had I done, he asked. Oh you know, a bit of general labouring, mixing cement, stacking and carrying bricks – all very technical stuff, obviously, and I had no idea what I was talking about. I just badly wanted to get this job. It was bullshit. I had never done any labouring of any kind, but it turned out that the three blokes already on the site were proper bricklayers, and that their regular labourer hadn't turned up for work. This meant that one of them would have to carry bricks and mix cement for the other two, which was a waste of a skilled bloke. If I could start right there and then, this fella said, I could have the job. Otherwise I could bugger off and stop wasting his time.

I have to say that it hadn't been my plan to start right there and then, and though I always looked like a total tramp I had on my 'chic-tramp' clothes as opposed to my actual tramp clothes. On the other hand something in me felt it was rather smart to go out and look for work and to start the same day, on a proper building site at that, and so I said yes.

In the unlikely event that it hadn't been obvious from the start, it became evident within about five minutes that I had no idea what I was doing. The good thing is that after I had asked the bloke to 'just remind me' what was the correct ratio of sand, cement and water to produce 'muck' (their charming name for the stuff that you put between bricks to make a wall) it turned out that to blend the required quantities in the cement mixer wasn't all that difficult. So I got off to a fairly decent start. I found that with Herculean effort I could just about manage to lift a bag of sand or cement to waist height and deposit the contents inside the upturned bowl of the machine, and that it wasn't all that hard to add enough water to produce something of workable consistency.

So far so good, but that was when the trouble started. The challenge now was how to get this huge quantity of churning gloop from the cement mixer, up a ladder and available for the three blokes who had at first been relieved not to have to do the labouring themselves, but were by now already becoming impatient that I was holding them up.

The answer, it turned out, was what is known as a 'hod' which is, for those of you who don't know, a little structure like three sides of an open metal box, on the end of a stick. The idea is that you prop this tool up against some surface, take a series of shovels-full of cement, and arrange them into this metal box in sort of layers, one on top of the other, until it is next to overflowing. A bit like making a lasagne. Then you hunker down so that your legs are bent and your shoulder is under the corner of the metal box containing the cement. The idea is that you straighten your legs, and thereby take the weight of the hod and cement on your shoulder. Do you have a mental picture of all this?

Well, where should I start? First of all, of course, there was no wall close enough to the cement mixer to prop the hod up against, and so I'm trying to put two wheelbarrows together to create a corner, but it should have been obvious that they were not going to be heavy or stable enough to prevent the hod from falling over once full. I have several tries, but every time I manage to pile up a few shovels-full of cement into it, it topples over, thereby slewing said cement over a wide radius. I glance upwards. The bricklayers don't know whether to laugh or cry. At the moment they are veering towards the former, but I know that the novelty won't last long and I badly don't want them to veer too far or fast towards being properly pissed off.

I'm not sure how I managed it, but eventually I found a way to keep this thing upright while I piled it up with cement and then, as directed, I reversed up underneath it, bent my knees, got my shoulder edged below the weight and proceeded to try to stand upright.

I thought the world was coming to an end right there and then.

At first I thought that it must be a joke. Someone was just having a laugh at my expense. I think I probably looked around to see if I could see the hidden cameras. At any moment Jonathan Routh (he of Candid Camera) would come out from hiding and invite me to join in the fun. It didn't happen. It wasn't a joke. It was all too real.

The general idea, as I understood it, was that I should take the entire weight of this metal box full of cement on my shoulder, and the fact was that I could scarcely raise it an inch off the ground. The pain was just short of screaming, and continued for half a minute even after I had put the thing back down on the ground.

Should I give up now? Even if I did manage to lift this particular load, the idea of being able to do this on a non-stop basis throughout the day was so far from reality that I might as well concede defeat right now. On the other hand, there were these three big tough blokes laughing their willies off at this poncey long-haired git of a student, and I was buggered if I was going to give them the satisfaction. At least not that easily. I tried again and, now more prepared for the consequences, by squeezing up my face and suppressing the urge to weep, I managed the take the weight of the thing and straighten my legs – at least for a moment.

I looked around in a daze, uncertain what to do now. All three brickies were up on the first floor of one of the houses, huge shiny trowels in hand, and waiting to get to work. Practically in unison, these blokes jerked their heads towards a ladder which was leaning against the scaffolding. Maybe it is only in my traumatised memory that they were whistling 'Hi ho, hi ho, it's off to work we go'. Who knows, but maybe that was the first ever occasion when I identified with Grumpy.

Not only did I have to endure the weight equivalent of a small car on my shoulder, but I also had to free one hand and use it to pull myself up a ladder to a level of about twelve feet off the ground. How the hell was I going to manage that? Has any of you tried to lift a Skoda on your shoulder? A small Fiat then? No, I didn't think so.

Not to extend the story too much, the point is that somehow I managed to wobble precariously up this ladder, holding on for dear life with one hand while the other tried to keep the burden of Sisyphus steady on my throbbing shoulder. Needless to say, generous proportions of the muck I was carrying slopped everywhere; over the edge of the hod, into my poofy flowing hair, behind my T-shirt and down my back. In any event, only a fraction of this precious substance made it with me to the summit.

I took each rung of the ladder one at a time, slowly, slowly, eventually reaching the top. Hillary and Tensing would have been proud. I walked carefully along the scaffolding planks to where these blokes were waiting to get on with their work. Beside them was a large wooden square, which was where this 'muck' needed to be deposited. So – how to get what remained of my first batch from my shoulder and on to this plate, without it going everywhere?

You have to understand that a hod even half-full of muck is incredibly top-heavy, and so the moment you allow it to tilt from the vertical, the weight of the contents will plummet to earth, with the attendant risk that it will slop wildly in whatever direction gravity is propelling it, rather than in a controlled way towards your required destination. And that's what happened. I managed to get the hod off my shoulder and standing upright on the ground like an upturned broom, but then as I tried to tip it gently in the direction of this wooden square where these blokes wanted it, the overwhelming weight took over and it tumbled out of control, slewing my hard-produced and miraculously-transported muck in all directions, and this time over the edge of the scaffolding and towards the ground twelve feet below. Excellent.

It's too late now to cut a long story short, but let's just say that eventually I got the hang of this, and after a while was managing to stumble up and down this bloody ladder with hods full of muck. I won't say that these three bricklayers got happy, and they certainly never stopped taking the piss, but after a while they did at least stop complaining.

The point for me was that at the end of the day, I was abso-bloody-lutely shattered. I'm talking about shattered like the

thing that happens when a bird hits a windscreen at seventy miles an hour. And I'm not talking about what happens to the windscreen (though that too). I'm talking about what happens to the bird.

The first thing I noticed was that the skin on my shoulder was worn away to what I felt certain must be the exposed bone. Sore, bright red, silently screaming a stream of obscenities along the lines of 'what the fuck …?' Suffice to say that the continual downward pressure on my puny frame made my spine feel as though it had been crushed by the weight of the moon.

My toe bones ached, my foot bones ached, my ankle bones ached, my shin bones ached, my knee bones ached – and for the first time in my life I understood how they were all connected and I could hear the words of the Lord. 'Give it up', He was shouting, 'before it's too late.'

At the end of this first day the bloke who hired me looked at me with something akin to pity, and was ready to give me some money, assuming that there was no way I was coming back tomorrow. However, I was young and I was foolhardy and I was proud and I was stupid. I was also hard up. I said I would, and by God I did.

When I got home at about 6 p.m., I was more or less unrecognisable from the bloke who had gone out at 8 a.m. that morning. My mother ran a bath for me (another expression I've never understood) and the gradual immersion reminded me of one of my earlier experiments with hallucinogenic drugs. I lay in the hot water, as stiff as a board, and thought I would never be able to move again.

The point is that this was the first day of actual work I had ever done in my short life. That one could really properly call work, as opposed to all that supposed reading or attending classes or lectures, holiday jobs, or even poncing about doing a bit of decorating for my Dad. The most that had ever amounted to was something along the lines of 'could you just see if you can hold the spirit level son?' This was real graft.

Guess what I learned? That you cannot work like that all day and every day. It is not possible for a human being to work flat out in that sort of way. You have to take time to lean on your shovel. And that if, as my mother so intensely feared, the country was going to the dogs, it was not these blokes who were propelling us in that undesirable direction.

A valuable lesson.

This is Your Life

O ne of the few redeeming features of being a Grumpy Old Man or Woman is that, in many cases, we have reached a stage in our lives when we are no longer looking for a job ourselves. We've been through that particular dark tunnel of vexation and most of us, thank God, are emerging out of the other side.

However, the bad news for any up-and-coming young person who is still applying for jobs is that the chances are there will be a grumpy old fart or two, like ourselves, involved in some way in the selection procedure.

So in case you find yourself in that unhappy situation, with one of us standing between you and your chosen career, it might be helpful to impart a few tips on how to minimise the irritation you are inevitably going to cause to a Grumpy. How to avoid pushing on as few as possible of the very many buttons which are likely to send him or her off on one, thereby inhibiting your otherwise uninterrupted progress towards greatness.

Probably the first thing to think about is your CV. Your 'Curriculum Vitae'. For therein lies a vast reservoir of potential to make our grump-making antennae start to twitch.

Up to the age of eighteen, Grumpy Old Men and Women had never heard of a CV. Actually, though in those days many of us

did a bit of it at school, it's fair to say that very few of us regularly used Latin words or phrases in our everyday speech. Unless of course we were David Cameron, in which case no doubt we did so all the time.

What else was there? Ad hoc? Sometimes, possibly. De facto? Sure, that's an irritating one, but probably not all that commonly used. Ibid? In even less frequent usage, I'd wager, and anyway, is some of that Greek? Anyway, I don't think there is anything quite to match CV. Curriculum Vitae. The programme or story of my life. A pretentious name for a pretentious thing, and maybe that's at the root of the reason why they seem to bring out the pretentiousness in so many people. If it's anything it should be 'LS' for life-story, but let's leave all that to one side and get on.

Not having given it a thought up to the age of about eighteen, from eighteen to twenty-five we probably thought a CV was a French car. We had no interest in our CVs, and certainly no thought that we ought to be doing fascinating things in order to make it look to a potential employer as though we were interesting people. To give ourselves a CV worth reading.

That was then. These days it seems that everyone has to have their CV. From school days, kids are evidently preoccupied with doing stuff 'that will look good on my CV'. It is emphasised to them by their teachers from a very early age. They have to have the sort of CV that will mark them out from the crowd, catch the eye of a potential employer, and secure them the first rung on the ladder to career success.

The difficult thing for young people in this situation is that the sort of stuff that they might easily think would make a favourable impression on an ordinary person, can so very easily have exactly the opposite effect if placed in front of a Grumpy. Indeed, can successfully get you so far up the nose of a Grumpy Old Man that they are no more inclined to invite you in for an interview than they are to want to share a towel with George Michael.

So, if you are to avoid the consequences which follow from irritating a Grumpy in authority, the first thing to think about when setting about your CV is the layout. My advice is to consider this carefully. I have often thought that you can tell more about a person by how they choose to lay out their CV than you can from the content of the CV itself.

The temptation is undoubtedly to dive into the repertoire of alternatives in your word-processing software, and to try to compose something that is going to catch the eye and mark you out from everyone else. It's an easy thing to give in to, and plenty of people do. The problem is that such a course is indeed likely to mark you out, but probably not in the way you have imagined.

Plunge into the internet, and there is no end of advice available about how to lay out the perfect CV. Not much of it is free, of course, and quite a few of the 175 million sites which come up within 0.06 seconds on Google offer to sort out your CV for you in exchange for some payment or other. Most of these sites tell you stuff that, if you can't work it out yourself, your problem is not about your CV. Your problem is that you are an eejit.

For example, the very first advice from the very first site to pop up in Google very helpfully warns you that:

Poor presentation can:

• Hide your most important information from the recruiter.

That's right. If, having worked so hard to achieve it, you forget to write down that you got a 1st Class Honours Degree at Cambridge, chances are that whoever reads the CV won't know about it.

• Stop your CV from being read fully.

So try to write it in the language spoken by the person who's going to read it.

• Build a negative impression of you in the mind of the recruiter.

Another useful tip, I think you'll agree. Mis-spell your own name and it won't get you off to a very good start.

• Convey to the recruiter that you would produce a poor standard of work.

If the CV reads like shit, maybe the work you do for the employer might be shit too? I would never have thought of that.

• Ultimately, STOP your application from going to the next stage.

Right again, a lousy CV means you might not get the job.

See what I mean? I won't go on to analyse the advice about what are the virtues of having good presentation, because I'm guessing that you can work those out for yourself.

The people who run these sites are probably the same people who offer to write a letter of complaint for you, or indeed to write to your employer asking for a pay-rise. The good thing about all these sites is that the advice about dealing with them is always the same. Don't.

Microsoft has also got a lot to answer for in this regard (and many others), by opening up such a range of extravagant and silly possibilities with their wild and wicked assortment of preposterous typefaces, bolds, italics and indentations.

The wankiest CVs are the ones where the name of the candidate is in some florid typeface, set out in bold, right in the middle of the front page …

Beresford Whinglett

… as if to say 'da dah! your prayers are answered, the messiah has arrived!'

If you want to avoid bringing a Grumpy out in hives, the best bet is to put your name in the same typeface as everything else, and position it on the left hand side of the page. Like so …

Beresford Whinglett

See? Even though it is presumably unavoidable that you have an idiotic name like Beresford Whinglett, at least you've done your level best to minimise the irritation for the rest of us by emblazoning it as though you are proud of the fact.

Then we're probably going to be treated to your address which, unless it is Eaton Square, Downing Street or The Mall, is going to be absolutely irrelevant, so short of putting it in an Olde English typeface, there's probably not that much you can do to mess that up.

The next crucial thing is the 'introductory statement'. You

know, the paragraph which some idiots place at the top of the page which is the literary equivalent of a fanfare, designed to make us feel very excited that we're holding your life-story in our hands. Again, I suspect that my industry is worse for this than most, but good heavens, have these people no shame?

'I am dynamic and an original thinker, who is also a creative self-starter with a strong track record of innovation and determination. I am articulate and an inspiring leader. I work well with people and am popular among my colleagues.' You probably think I'm making this up but I assure you that this isn't the half of it. Some of them stop short of 'I am God's gift to television and anyone who can't see that and doesn't want to hire me needs bi-focals' – but not all of them.

This phenomenon is not unlike what goes on with all those complete know-nothings who audition for *The X Factor* or whatever it is – total geeks who stand there looking like a badly drawn cartoon of a nerd and tell the panel – with no obvious sense of irony that – 'I have talent, I have charisma, and I have a wonderful voice.' Then they make a noise like fingernails scraping across the blackboard (remember that?) and are stunned to learn that the panel's tears don't seem to be because they think they've just discovered the musical equivalent of a cure for cancer. When they're told that they're 'not going to London', not only are they in tears, but their mothers are in tears, their fathers and grandparents are in tears, their brothers and sisters are in tears, and the only person trying to suppress a smile is the fat girlfriend who had to come along for the ride but as sure as hell was going to get dumped the second he looked like making the big time.

A variation on this theme, which invariably creases me up, is when this introductory paragraph is written in the third person. 'Beresford Whinglett is beloved by his colleagues, admired for his talent and modesty, is a credit to his parents and to the Empire, and can feed 5,000 people with five loaves and two fishes.' When

I see this I always want to ask the candidate the question 'Who wrote your CV?', and sometimes I do. Usually they think I'm trying to catch them out in some way and reply that of course they wrote it. So I ask who wrote the opening paragraph, and invariably they say that they did. So I point out that it's a bit odd to talk about yourself as though you were someone else, which leaves them flummoxed. I know, I know, you're thinking what a bastard I am and you're right; in my defence I'd only say that I have only ever done this with the most appallingly conceited plonkers.

Sometimes when I come across one of these CVs with the outrageous introductory build-up, I am almost tempted to invite the applicant just out of curiosity, to see if they will exhibit any embarrassment in having to actually meet someone in front of whom they've made themselves such a prince among dorks. But of course, that would be self-defeating, because if that happened they would have achieved their objective by getting my attention in the first place. So I don't.

However, I have sometimes been on interview panels where I played no part in selecting the short-list, and so found myself meeting people who had written this sort of bullshit. In such cases I have always found it reassuring to confirm that anyone who comes over as an egocentric toss-pot in their CV, always turns out to be one in real life. Always.

If you want to avoid pissing off Grumpy Old Men and Women who may be part of the selection procedure, the rule is very simple and very easy to take on board. It's this: the more florid a style you choose, the more of a pretentious ponce you are. Easy as that. The more you put stuff in bold, or underline, or use italics, the more you are making a twot of yourself. Give them the benefit of the doubt and assume they can work out which are the important bits without you having to put them in some exotic script. Make it clear and unassuming. That's my advice. Take it or leave it.

So having discussed the style and layout of your CV, what about the content? And in particular, what is it OK to invent, and what should you try to tell the truth about?

The other day I read an article in the newspaper which suggested that something like two-thirds of people admit to enhancing their CV. I think this is a polite way of saying that they made stuff up. Wow. Two out of three people are bloody liars. So few!

I guess that I probably shouldn't be overly surprised by this. One former colleague of mine told me recently that she used to add an 'O' level or an 'A' level every time she applied for a job. Eventually she got so used to the idea that she had passed ten 'O' levels that she started to believe it herself. By this stage, aged about thirty-eight, she had falsified her exam results so frequently that she genuinely could not remember how many 'O' levels she had actually passed.

Though I find this a bit shocking, I don't especially mind all that much, because I reckon that any potential employer who cares how many 'O' and 'A' levels a candidate has passed, or believes what he sees on the CV, probably deserves everything he gets. What I do tend to care about a little more is people who lie about what they've done since.

This is also particularly notorious in the television industry because there is so much scope for making stuff up. If you were working at a TV production company when a particular series was being made, it's fairly easy to say that you worked on it in some capacity or other. Maybe someone on the production asked you one day to run out and find out what variety of bagels they sold at the local deli – well that could easily count in some people's minds as 'researcher'. Maybe you were asked to order a cab for the producer one day – well honestly, how far is that really from having actually been the 'production coordinator'?

The best, or worst, example of this that ever happened to me was a candidate for a job who claimed to have been a researcher on an episode of *World in Action* which, in fact, I had produced. I had never met or heard of this woman before. This is a true story. When, some way through the interview, I asked what she had done on the production, it turned out that the person who had *actually* been the researcher had asked her to spend a day tracking down some newspaper cuttings. So that was enough, in her mind, to justify the claim that she had been the 'researcher' on the programme. I know that this was OK in her mind because, even when the deception was uncovered, she didn't seem embarrassed.

So on we go then, ploughing through the CV. The next thing is your career to date. Do you put your jobs in chronological order, starting with your paper round at the age of nine, in which case the reader might well be forgiven for falling asleep before you get to your current employment some pages later? Or do you start with your current job, and then go backwards? And if so, how far backwards do you go?

My advice is that if you are under the age of Grumpiness – say thirty-five – you should start with your current job and go backwards and include everything. If you are in your Grumpy years, you might want to stop a bit earlier. That your first job was delivering telegrams in the 1960s may be of interest and impress other Grumpies. However, you may find the younger ones looking at you like you are a character out of Dickens. Not least because most of them won't know what a telegram was.

Usually it's also a fairly good idea to give a little summary of what the job entailed, especially if the job title can be a bit misleading. And here, as elsewhere, there is a strong and obvious temptation to enhance your role in running the company, which is to be avoided at all costs.

I once interviewed a bloke from BT whose job title was 'Account Manager', but whose job description left me thinking that if we did hire him I'd better cancel my BT account because there could be no doubt that the whole company would collapse without him. God knows what the other 29,000 employees must have been doing, as this bloke seemed to do everything. Needless to say, he didn't get the job, but on reflection I think maybe he must have been speaking the truth and got a job elsewhere. Have you tried to get anyone from BT to answer the phone recently?

This can also work in reverse. Job-title inflation has meant that many people are called very exalted things when in reality, if they failed to turn up to work, it would take three months before anyone else noticed. This is particularly true in American companies where everyone from the tea-boy upwards is called 'vice-president' of something or other.

When I first saw this title on a business card, I thought the person must be vice-president in the way that Lyndon Johnson was Vice-President, ready to step nimbly into the boss's shoes if he or she is mercilessly slain and left bleeding on the sidewalk. In fact it turns out that most big US corporations have about 1,000 people called 'vice-president' and in many cases the actual president wouldn't recognise them in the lift.

After your education and career, the next and possibly most important section of your CV is dedicated to 'Hobbies and Interests'.

I always had trouble with that, did you? In the very early days, when these things mattered to me, I used to scan my mind to see if I could think of anything that interested me other than pursuing women. The truth is that, at the age we're talking about, there was no subject of interest other than pursuing women. And even if I had had any other interest, I wouldn't have had the time to pursue it because all my spare time was already committed to pursuing women. But as it wasn't an option to put down 'pursuing women' in the space, and leaving it blank wasn't an option either, what were the choices?

You could take a risk and say something exotic like astronomy or something posh like antiques, but the trouble is that there is always a chance that if you ever get as far as the interview, someone on the panel is going to know something about the subject, and then you can be totally and royally screwed.

Can you imagine anything worse? Your experience of skin-diving extends to having watched a lot of *Sea Hunt* with Lloyd Bridges on the telly when you were a kid, but you think you might get away with putting it down on your CV. Then it turns out that one of the blokes interviewing you is an up-and-coming bloody Jacques Cousteau and wants to talk about it. It's going to become obvious to him in about half a minute that you don't have the slightest idea what you're talking about, and at that point you will probably want to eat your own head.

So I used to be cautious and stick to 'reading', which didn't seem too reckless because I was an English graduate. I also used

to write 'cinema' which I think is supposed to mean that you're a fan of all those old black-and-white movies with Orson Welles or Polish films which consist of little rubber men being chased by skyscrapers. What I meant was that I'd been to see *Papillon* or *Butch Cassidy and the Sundance Kid* at the local fleapit. With luck, I wouldn't be asked, but if I was I reckoned that I could busk my way through it without being totally humiliated.

Under sports you could write down 'eventing' or 'croquet', which will immediately put you down as an aristocrat or a former deputy leader of the Labour party. If you put down 'round the world yacht-racing' they'll probably admire you but not expect to see you in the office much. Most people these days seem to put down skiing, which they think marks them out as trendy and sporty and one of the in-crowd, and just makes me think this is someone who's going to be spending a lot of time that they really should be at work, in hospital.

Same with mountaineering, orienteering or caving. They might be able to tell an entertaining anecdote during the coffee break, but don't expect to see them much, and when you do they'll most likely be on crutches.

In the old days I also used to be able to put down 'running' and 'tennis', and then more latterly I found it sensible to change those to 'walking' and 'tennis'. It wasn't that I still played tennis, but I still watched it on the telly, so I reckoned that counted.

Sitting on the grumpy side of the desk in more recent times, I've realised that my qualms about inventing hobbies and interests were over-sensitive. Over the years I've come across candidates who declared themselves to be active in local politics and it turned out that they had voted in the last by-election, people who boasted of being interested in travel who had taken a weekend break to Disneyland in Paris, and one rather wonderful bloke who wrote down 'taxidermy' and whose attempt at an explanation revealed that he didn't completely understand what the word meant, and consequently it ended up ... well, I think you can complete the feeble joke for yourself.

Application forms

Anyway, in the end it doesn't actually matter how inventive or comprehensive is your CV, because about a week after you've sent it off by email or letter, notwithstanding that you have outlined everything they could possibly need to know clearly, concisely and in as much detail as could possibly be necessary, the next thing that will land on your in-box or door-mat will be an application form.

You've got to fill in the application form. It matters not how impressive or erudite or thorough your letter of application might have been, or how much detail you've put on your CV, still you've got to fill in the form. It's the law.

I'm not sure about Grumpy Old Women, but Grumpy Old Men aren't very good at forms. Filling them out, I mean. We're not very good at forms in general.

Obviously, as with CVs, it's a long time since most of us have filled out a job application form. However, we still have to fill out plenty of other forms, even if it's only to apply for our pensions, or residents' parking permits, or plots in the graveyard, and they always irritate beyond endurance.

To start with, a form feels to us like it's an official document, and we don't like official documents because we don't like officials and we don't like officiousness. To put it more generally, Grumpies don't really like bureaucracy at all. But here is this document, a few pieces of paper, a template, which requires us to summarise our lives into a standard form. Once again we're being processed, and we hate to be processed.

The form asks us to write down our details in a series of little boxes, all of a given size and shape, so that we can be categorised, put into files, analysed into statistics, considered, mulled over, and popped into this pile or into that pile. Usually by someone who has never met us. Someone just looking at the words in the boxes.

This is their opportunity to ask us all those questions like 'ethnic origin', and we have to tick one of a series of euphemisms. I don't know why they need to know this, especially not at this point, and one cannot help but wonder if it isn't actually a way of avoiding the embarrassment of inviting a black person for an interview when the employer is certain they're only going to hire a white person. Presumably none of this was necessary when a black person was called Mtoto and so the racist employer could filter him out well before the interview stage. What must have happened is that too many people named Prendergast were invited for interview and turned out to be that off-shoot of the Prendergast family from Malawi. So racists need to ask at the application-form stage in order to avoid embarrassment all round.

Interestingly they also put down a space on the application form for 'date of birth', so why do you think they need to know this? Since employers are not allowed to discriminate on the basis of sex, race or age, why is this relevant, do you think? For the answer, see above. It saves everyone from wasting their time interviewing a dinosaur when they are looking for an embryo.

Anyway there it is, probably the size of an A2 sheet, folded down the middle to allow four sides of A4 paper, surely enough for you to be able to write down everything they need to know about you.

The advice I always gave to the kids when they were growing up, but have never taken myself then or now, is to read the whole form before you start filling it in. Like you used to have to do with your exam papers when it said 'answer 4 questions'. This is the only way to prevent yourself from writing down your full name in the box marked 'name', only to find that the next box says 'first name'. The only way to know that they don't want your whole address in the box marked 'address' because there is a separate box just below marked 'post-code'. How many times have you done that? And how much of a prat does it make you look? But does that make any difference to you next time? No, of course it doesn't. Because we know better.

Date of birth – well yes, usually I can remember my date of birth, but usually I put the day where the month should be, or the month where the day should be, or if it wants me to write the year in full – '1836' by the time I've realised that I've usually written '36, or vice versa.

So anyway, just as with your CV, you have to fill out, in exquisite detail, the schools you have attended, the exams you passed, the grades, the further education, the passes and grades again. All fairly straightforward, unless of course you want to make up a few exam passes, in which case the trick is just to ensure that whatever you write matches what you wrote on your CV.

The Interview

C asting my mind back for 30 years or so, the first proper interview I ever had was with the BBC for a job as a graduate journalist trainee after I had finished at university.

In those days we called a university a university, unless we were posh in which case we called it 'varsity' or unless we were very posh indeed in which case we talked about 'going up'. These days they call it 'uni', even though for the most part 'uni' is what we used to call 'poly' – but we won't go into that now because that's another thing.

This was the seventies, and in those days none of us thought too much about things as dull as careers. We were young and hip. Across the Atlantic Dr Timothy Leary was urging people to 'tune in, turn on, and drop out' which amounted to an exaltation to reject the ways of 'the man' and to do a lot of recreational drugs. So, if we were upper class with rich and long-suffering parents, we were popping off to San Francisco and following Timothy's advice. Oddly enough, I met Timothy Leary many years later, and though it was a great pleasure to do so I did come away with the feeling that he must have taken rather too much of his own counsel. Anyway, that's by the way. The choice of dropping out and heading off to the west coast of America was an option for only the very privileged few.

If we were middle class we might still head off to Ibiza, and even if we were plebs we might get as far as St Ives. If all that failed, you could still feel cool by going down to Hyde Park for the Stones concerts or to the Isle of Wight to see Marsha Hunt – all hair and hot-pants – or Jimi. It was all hippy communes and sharing whatever we had and a little light marijuana. We'd set up the stereo with the speakers as far apart as the wires would permit and then marvel at how the guitar chords from 'Whole Lotta Love' would seem to come from opposite sides of the room. Were we cool or what?

The very idea of being ambitious was counter-cultural. The correct response if anyone ever asked the dreaded question 'What do you want to do?' was a flick of the waist-length hair and a shrug of the rounded shoulders. It certainly was not trendy to be a careerist.

With that in mind, I had studied English at Newcastle University which, of course, made me as cool as cool could be because it qualified me for absolutely nothing. Unless of course I planned to go door to door, offering to explain the hidden meanings behind various great works of literature, but I guessed that there might not be a lot of call for it. So I think it's fair to say that when eventually I turned up at the Careers Office, they didn't appear to be all that thrilled to see me.

I seem to think that they had a few fading leaflets about a high-flying career in the civil service, but the bloke with the Sherlock Holmes pipe and Moriarty attitude didn't seem very encouraging. 'They only want Oxbridge types for that sort of thing', and you can gauge my level of worldliness in those days by the fact that I think I knew where Oxford was and I think I knew where Cambridge was, but thought it better not to reveal my ignorance by letting on that I had no idea where Oxbridge was.

'I was thinking of applying to the BBC.'

I can still hear the snort reverberating over the airwaves between thirty-odd years ago and now.

'Well you can try but honestly I don't think you've got a cat's chance in hell.' Yes, that was a modern expression then, and also is what passed for encouragement in the Careers Dept of Newcastle University.

He rifled through a series of big metal filing cabinets and eventually retrieved some fading and crumbling four-year-old application forms for something called the 'Graduate Journalist Trainee Scheme', but they only took twelve people a year and they were all toffs. I may not have known where Oxbridge was but I knew what a toff was, and I knew that I wasn't one of them. Anyway what the hell ...

So I won't tell you the whole story, but let's just say that to his and my amazement I was invited down to London for what was described as 'a preliminary interview'. I think my parents must have been kindly trying to manage my expectations because their comment was something along the lines of 'never mind, you've done well even to have got an interview', which I think was probably my attitude as well. All good for experience when you come to get your actual job – presumably in the local insurance office. An early example of the maxim 'experience is what you get when you don't get what you want'.

I knew nothing about interviews for jobs except that I probably worked out for myself that one ought to look smart and not drop your Hs or slurp your tea. These days, if a kid turned up for an interview at my company and said he didn't watch a lot of telly, I'd throw him out without even asking him another question, but for some reason it didn't occur to me for a moment that if I had any sense I would watch some telly or listen to a lot of radio by way of preparation,

On reflection I think the two rather pleasant people who interviewed me were probably as much as anything amused and intrigued to meet somebody so stupid as to turn up at an interview at the BBC without having made a recent study of some of their programmes. It turned out that I had never listened to *The World at One* or *PM*, hadn't seen the evening TV news for some time, and wouldn't have been able to find the World Service on the dial. On the other hand I could give them a fairly detailed appraisal of their 'world news in two minutes', which was broadcast with an irritating ripple of electronic music behind it every hour on the hour on Radio 2, and the same service, but lasting only a minute with still more irritating music behind it, on the half hour on Radio 1. I suspect, in fact, that as well as distinguishing myself as an idiot, I was also distinguished by being the only person to be interviewed who had listened to what at the time would have been considered so trivial an aspect of their service.

Maybe it was just curiosity on their part but, amazingly, I was invited back for a second interview. The first one having been so pleasant and, apparently, so easy, it still didn't occur to me that the second one would be any different. It's odd to think of how catastrophically thick I must have been not to have realised that the absence of any real opinions about their programmes might be a disadvantage. Call it the arrogance of youth, or call it calamitous stupidity. It was probably a bit of both, but anyhow I turned up at Broadcasting House feeling bright and breezy. I think I probably knew enough to know that I should read the newspapers that day and maybe have an answer to a question about 'what story should we be leading on this evening?' but I didn't know much else.

To my utter astonishment, I was ushered into a room with one chair on my side of a long table, and eight chairs and eight people on the other. I think it's fair to say that I had never been so terrified in my short life, including my first visit to the mortuary, and I assumed there must be some misunderstanding. Maybe I had stumbled by mistake into the interview panel for the next Director General. I didn't know enough about any subject under the sun to sustain a cross-examination by this group of people, let alone about journalism or broadcasting. They would be able to exhaust my knowledge of news and current affairs in about eighteen seconds.

I think it honestly occurred to me to say 'I think there has been some mistake' and make for the door, and I'd like to suggest that it was bravery which made me stay. More probably it was cold inertia brought on by terror. A rabbit in the headlights.

They asked me to sit down, and then they introduced themselves. There was a bloke from the Home Service with a very senior-sounding title, and a bloke from the World Service with an even more impressive handle. There was a bloke from TV News and a bloke from Radio News and a bloke from 'the sequences' and a woman from Personnel. All of these people were straight out of central casting, looking like journalists in the same way that the cast of The Lavender Street Mob looked like villains. Several wore cardies, one wore a sports jacket with leather patches on the arms, and one was smoking a pipe. And it seemed to me that all they wanted to do was to prove to each other how clever they were by making a little prat like me look like what I was; a presumptuous little git.

At this vantage point, some thirty-odd years later, I really don't think I can remember much about what they asked me. Or maybe the humiliation has filtered it out of my hard-drive. I recall it as a blur, and I genuinely don't think that it's possible that I gave them a decent answer to anything.

What did I think of the current situation in Rhodesia? I hardly knew where Rhodesia was. Did I think there was a case for a change in the blasphemy laws? Good God, how would I know? Did I think that Harold Wilson was about to call an election? And just remind me who Harold Wilson is …?

Well obviously it wasn't quite that bad, but I don't think it was all that far off.

After about an hour of this, the ordeal was over, and I distinctly remember coming out of the boardroom, leaning back against the wall and exhaling loudly and with obvious relief. I was sweating like a man who had been trapped in a sauna wearing a deep-sea diver's outfit. The secretary looked at me with pity and concern. There was a pause, and I think she must have felt a wave of compassion, because she looked around as if to ensure that no-one was listening before she spoke: 'Oh I wouldn't worry too much about that. You're the first person who has come out of there this morning who hasn't been in tears.'

To the astonishment of myself, my family, and certainly the bloke in the Careers Office, I got the gig. God knows why. I genuinely think someone must have pointed out that everyone on this course since it started had a familiar sounding surname, and that a bit of positive discrimination in favour of an oik might be advisable. The only possible alternative explanation is that the whole interviewing panel had all been fired that morning, and wanted to pull a practical joke on the Corporation on their way out. Whatever the reason, I was joining the BBC, and that was undoubtedly the single biggest break I ever had in my professional life.

All that was of course a very long time ago, and we should come right up to date so that our always helpful Grumpy perspective can be of some use to anyone going for an interview today. Since Grumpies are, for the most part, too old to be going to a lot of job interviews, I think the most useful thing we can do here is once again to switch to the point of view of the poor little bugger who wants a job and is likely to find a Grumpy Old Man or Woman on the other side of the table. What can you do in order to decrease the likelihood that you will vex the Grumpy on whose acquiescence you may need to rely?

The first thing is that you have to decide what to wear. I was going to write a whole load of stuff here about 'nothing too ostentatious' and all that, but if I'm entirely honest all that is a complete waste of time. One thing about Grumpy Old Men in particular is that very few of us take a blind bit of notice of how we dress ourselves, and so are very unlikely to care too much about whatever you are wearing. I think the trick is not to look as though you are going to a disco, and not to look as though you are going to the royal enclosure at Ascot. If you are the wrong person for the job, turning up looking like Prince Charles isn't going to cut it for you. On the other hand if you are the right person for the job, you'll probably get it if you don't turn up looking like Grayson Perry.

For a woman I think the conventional advice used to be something like, wear what you'd wear if you were going to meet your boyfriend's parents on an autumn day. Nothing too tight. Nothing too loose. Nothing too colourful, and certainly nothing too sexy. I know that I am simply asking to make myself the subject of obloquy here, but in the spirit of total honesty which characterises these books I should admit that I have actually rejected female candidates for jobs on the grounds that they were too sexy. I know, I know, but I have done this on what I regard as the very legitimate grounds that none of the guys in the office would get any work done. I can almost feel any female readers bristling, and I'm guessing that these days it's probably against the law, but I really don't think this is unreasonable. And if you do, all I can say is, get over it.

If this was one of those proper little instruction books about how to make a good impression on an employer or whatever, I'd be adding stuff now like 'don't be late for the interview', or 'shine your shoes', but it's not, so I won't.

The next question is, how to prepare for what they are going to ask you at the interview. We've already demonstrated from my interview at the BBC how not to do it. If you're not going to have the elementary common sense to find out a bit about the people you want to work for, then better not to turn up to the interview at all.

On the other hand, sometimes they are going to ask you stuff you should have been able to anticipate and mug up about, and sometimes they are not. I had a colleague at Granada, for example, who used to begin every interview for anyone applying for a job as a researcher by asking them to name every member of the Cabinet. In the unlikely event that they could do so, he would ask them if they could name every member of the Shadow Cabinet. If they could do that, he didn't want to ask them anything else. He reckoned that this told him everything he needed to know about the candidate, and he hired them. If not, not. But what a bastard, eh?

However, leaving aside the wholly cantankerous Grumpy whose mischief and malevolence may know no bounds, and therefore for whose questions it is impossible to prepare, what are some of the more predictable things you might be asked at an interview?

Well an obvious one is 'Why do you want to come and work for us?' and the smart-arsed answer is because you've heard what a great company it is, and/or you've always wanted to work here since you were a small boy. This is a bit creepy, but if that's going to be your answer, obviously you need to have done the homework, and at least to know that the company actually existed when you were a small boy. Personally I prefer it if people tell the truth – something like, 'The fact is I don't really want to work at all, but if I have to, you guys seem as good as anyone', or better still, 'Actually my boyfriend works at the printer around the corner and we thought we could get the bus together'.

Another of the classic questions is 'Where do you see yourself in five years time?' and one of the classic answers to that is

'Sitting where you are and doing your job', which is quite cute, and quite smart, and therefore quite irritating. However, if you are going to say this to a Grumpy, I should warn you that there is a fair chance that it took him twenty years to get to where he is today, and the idea that you're going to get there in five might seem a little arrogant.

I think the single biggest misunderstanding between interviewer and interviewee is the importance attached to the inevitable final question, 'Do you have any questions for us?' Whenever I have heard anyone from what I believe we these days are required to call the 'Human Resources' department talk about these things, they always describe this as the interviewing-board equivalent of the 'hobbies and interests' section of the application form. You are obliged, apparently, to show what an interesting and thoughtful person you are by asking some perceptive and penetrating question about the job.

Having been an interviewer far more frequently than an

'interviewed' I can tell you for certain that, by the time you get to that stage of the interview, all they want to do is to go for their lunch, or go for a wee, or head off for a cup of tea. They've probably already seen half a dozen people that morning and all of them have tried to impress by asking some clever-dick question which, out of politeness, they have to have a stab at answering. Take it from me. When you are asked this question at the end of the interview, the answer they want to hear from you is 'No thank you very much. I think I understand everything I need to', so that they can get on with something useful.

So there you are. If you think you might find yourself on the other side of the table being interviewed by a Grumpy, these are a few of the things you should commit to memory. Find out something about the company you are applying for, try not to look like too much of a prat, and try not to show off too much. Other than that, you're on your own. What did you expect?

Instruction Manuals

S o at last you've actually managed to get a job and, like all bright-eyed, shiny-faced, good, responsible young adults, more than anything else, you want to do well. You so want to do well.

Maybe you might be tempted to feel that, in order to give yourself the best chance of excelling, you should avail yourself of one of those advice books written by some guru or other, on how to get on and prosper in this new and strange world that you are entering.

While it goes against the grain for us to do anything so mundane as actual research when preparing the Grumpy books, on this occasion I thought that we might stretch a point and take a look at some of the competition for the attention and money of anyone seeking wisdom about how to deal with the world of work.

Thus it was that the other day I found myself with twenty minutes or so to spare before a meeting in Piccadilly and thought I'd go into one of the large bookshops in the area to have a scout around. Blimey! If you haven't already done the same thing yourself you will, I assure you, be utterly amazed by the dozens and dozens of volumes dedicated to various aspects of the daily grind. I mean there are hundreds of them.

In this particular store there was a whole section dedicated to work. Bigger than the section designated to travel, twice the size of the section dedicated to art, and three times the size of the section on science. All these acres and acres of print about boring old work.

In most cases even the titles tell us enough to know that we'd rather contract a severe case of St Vitus' Dance than to open the first page. Here's a sample of the more engaging:

The Jelly Effect: How to Make Your Communication Stick

The No Asshole Rule: Building a Civilised Workplace and Surviving One That Isn't

Eat That Frog!: Get More of the Important Things Done, Today!

Who Moved My Cheese?: An Amazing Way to Deal with Change in Your Work and in Your Life

And finally, my favourite of all, entitled:

Screw It, Let's Do It: Lessons in Life by Sir Richard Branson

Like I say, there are hundreds of these volumes, but they seem to fall into three basic categories. They are either supposed to be funny, in which case the clue is that they have a hilarious title and some sort of a cartoon on the front cover.

Alternatively they come under the heading of 'a blinding glimpse of the obvious' in which case they probably still have a cartoon on the cover, but maybe have a more serious sub-title, like 'the definitive guide to coping with your boss'.

The third category are books which seem to be written by the equivalent of the school creep who has passed his own exams with flying colours and, rather than getting on with his life or proceeding about his business, wants to show off what a clever dick he is. Loads of these are of the 'I've made a million, so you can too' variety, which just make you think that if following his money-making scheme also turned you into the smug little wanker that he's turned into, you'd be better off remaining poverty stricken.

We won't go into a comprehensive review of all of these books because that would involve actual work and life's too short. However, it is worth picking out just one or two of their general features.

The Joy of Work for example is one that I assume is supposed to be funny. I assume that because it has a cartoon on the front cover, and a superficially attractive sub-title *Guide to finding happiness at the expense of your co-workers*. This book actually starts off with the side-splitting premise that once your company has taken away everything it can from you (by putting you in an open-plan office), the only things left are *'the floor, the ceiling, and your happiness'*. It then posits the view that taking away the floor is not really practical because that would involve digging a hole to Australia. They are unlikely to take away the ceiling, it says, because then the workers in the floors above would fall on your head. So that the only thing left for the company to take away is your happiness, and this is a book designed to prevent it from doing so. Are you with me so far? Helpful, eh?

The Joy of Work is full of advice in little boxes and cartoons, as well as some practical recommendations. You can know everything you need to know about it by reference to just one suggestion which is that you can undermine your current boss by changing your religion to that of your boss's boss so that you can attend the same church. See what I mean? An imminent threat to your ability to stay dry, and practical too.

Under the heading 'a blinding glimpse of the obvious' one can fr'instance another appealing title, which is *Is Your Boss Mad?* On the cover of the edition I looked at there is a picture of a woman who looks like a cross between Julie Andrews and Petula Clark, but who may be screaming and may be the author. If she is both, she must be screaming in her joy and amazement that anyone is prepared to part with a cover price of £13 to read over 200 pages of horse-shit. It includes helpful suggestions such as *'Arrive on Time: if you always arrive late because the train you normally take means you cannot get to work on time, get an earlier one, even if it means arriving at work very early.'* See what I mean? I just picked that one at random, but every page seems to be littered with similar pearls. Another example would be about learning to deal with pressure. The advice is to *'Be helpful. Be friendly. Be firm.'* I'm not making this up; go and look for yourself. Honestly, there is one on every page. On 'Mistakes', it suggests that you *'find out your boss's attitudes towards mistakes',* including *'Have they ever made a mistake?'* and *'How did they learn?'*

OK, so my overall feeling is that if you have bought and are reading 'Is Your Boss Mad?' you've wasted your money because the kind of help you need is available free of charge on the NHS.

But it must be the case that some people want to know what these lard-heads have to say, otherwise there wouldn't be so many of them being published. I picked up another one called *The Rules of Work*. On the face of it, this seems to be a serious volume. It claims to be an 'international bestseller' and its cover doesn't even suggest a hint of comedy. However, a glance inside clearly demonstrates a talent for satire.

For examples one of 'The Rules of Work' is *'Cultivate a Smile'*. But not just any old smile, apparently. *'Look in the mirror and smile. Chances are it will look wrong. Of course it will. You can only see yourself front on. And photos don't work either. They're in 2D and there is a lot missing when you look at them. You need to see your smile from all angles – in 3D – and there is only one way to see that and that is on film – video or whatever.'* The book goes on to suggest that you set up the video recorder and shoot yourself from all angles, testing out your smile. My guess is that you'd be

Smiles in 3D

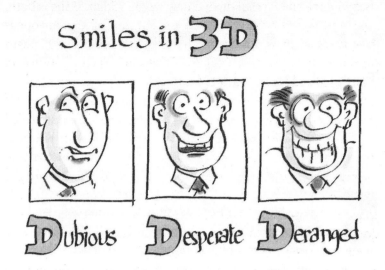

Dubious   **Desperate**   **Deranged**

better off just shooting yourself.

Leaving aside the fact that I'm not sure that your average film or video allows you to see yourself in 3D, what on earth can this bloke be on about? His closing advice is *'to improve your smile make sure you aren't doing a lop-sided grin, that your teeth can be seen but not too much … keep practicing until you get it right.'* And this book costs over ten quid!

I could go on about this for ages – honestly, there is no end of old rubbish available for anyone who is sufficiently gullible and hapless to buy it. However, in exchange for whatever price you've paid for this book, let me give you a single and priceless piece of absolutely reliable advice. Don't buy any of these business self-help books. Every single word, of every single one of them, is bullshit. Trust me.

The First Day

 ery few things in life are as stressful as your first day in a new job.

It doesn't matter how many jobs you have had before, or how often you move around, the first day is always going to be a pain in the tush.

For one thing it's your first day, so on this day of all days you've got to get there on time. You've sat up the night before and planned your route – by bus, tube and train, or by bus, train and a walk, or by car, train, bus and a walk – but still you may not be absolutely sure of the least irritating way to get there. And you don't want to leave anything to chance, so you end up leaving home at about six in the morning and getting there about two hours earlier than you needed to.

This is therefore going to be your opportunity to identify the nearest coffee bar, make friends with the local newsagent (or more probably the people sleeping in their doorways), walk around the neighbourhood or catch up with a little light reading for a couple of hours. A great start to the day.

You don't want to seem too much of a creep in front of your new colleagues so you wait until five minutes before starting time and head into work. Only at this point do you discover that the front entrance doesn't open for another hour and that

employees go in through the tradesman's entrance which is in
the street round the back. And it's raining. So having originally
turned up two hours early, you're actually going to get there ten
minutes late and soaked to the skin.

Then there is the wait in the foyer for the woman from HR
who is going to show you to exactly where you'll be working. Is
there any feeling quite like the one you get from being looked up
and down by a group of people who all know each other but are
clapping eyes on you for the first time? The long walk between
the desks and filing cabinets and coffee machines and corridors. It's like the Green Mile, and you can almost hear the
inmates clanking their mugs against the bars. All the guys are

wondering whether you are competition for the attention of either the boss or for Bethany or Babs or whoever is the babe-most-coveted in this particular establishment. Meanwhile all the women are sizing you up as what I recently came to learn is currently called 'top totty' (yes, blokes too, apparently), or more probably writing you off as too ugly, too lowly, or too much of a dweeb to be of consequence.

All of that applies up to the age of about thirty-five, of course. Up to the point, in fact, when you may well be entering your Grumpy years. If you start a new job any time from the age of about thirty-five onwards you will find that none of the above applies. The only thing you have to get used to after the age of about thirty-five is that you are gradually disappearing altogether, so that by the time you are aged about forty-five, no-one else in the office can see you at all. You aren't any threat to anyone else's prospects of promotion, and you certainly aren't any threat to the younger blokes who are trying to impress Bethany or Babs. You are irrelevant in all material respects, over the hill, past it. You are, indeed, invisible, and therefore Grumpy.

However that's a long way off for the moment.

Everything about your first day is awful. You don't know where your desk is or where the boss's desk is. You don't know where you go for tea, coffee or a doughnut. You don't know where the men's room is, and you don't know who to ask where the men's room is, and you don't know whether they call it 'the men's room'. Worse than any of that is the fact that you are going to be introduced to about a hundred people, and you aren't going to remember the names of any of them, with the possible exception of Bethany and Babs, who are both looking at you in the way that Caesar's wife looked at fresh Christians – and wondering what you'll look like once chewed up and spat out.

When I first started working at the BBC I was living in an upstairs flat in West Dulwich and working at Television Centre in

White City. So just about an hour and a half of commuting each way by train and tube. That was on a good day when the trains and tubes ran on time or ran at all. Such days were in the minority. It didn't really matter though because we often worked 'til after the late news which in those days was on BBC2, so I more or less had no choice but to use my car, which at that time was a ten-year-old VW beetle in a neat combination of beige and rust. Driving to work meant that the commute was closer to two hours in the mornings, though a lot less at night, and obviously there was nowhere nearby to park.

In those days there were two news-teams working in parallel alongside each other – one on BBC1 and one on BBC2. I was directed to the Television Newsroom in the Spur, which was an annexe off the main circle which is BBC TV Centre. It's hard to believe it, but the people recruited to the Graduate Trainee Scheme in those days were thought to be potential Channel Controllers or Directors-General, so in some respects we were treated quite well. This privilege also further exacerbated the resentment which was already present among other colleagues who had got their jobs in the newsroom the hard way – usually after having worked for years on a provincial newspaper.

One aspect of this privileged treatment was that, on our first day in TV news, we were invited up for a drink with the Head of News. The Head of News at the time was a ferocious man whose name I can remember but am not going to reveal because he is dead now and the following story doesn't reflect on him all that well. Anyway, the thing was that this little reception took place in an office at the front of Television Centre where the statue of Arial stands, and from which you can see across the circle towards the front entrance of the site.

As I stood there, glass in hand, talking to the Head of News, I looked out of the window and saw a Ford Granada drive straight through the barrier, smashing it into pieces. The car squealed to a halt, and three men wearing ski masks got out and started belabouring the security men around the head and necks with what looked like baseball bats. Nearby a security van was presumably delivering the wages, or whatever. Entirely alarmed at what I was seeing, I looked to the Head of News for my cue about what to do. He seemed unperturbed.

'These fucking drama people,' he said without any trace of excitement or interest whatsoever. 'When will they learn that they need to warn us when they are pulling off their little stunts? Someone could easily get frightened with all that going on.'

I didn't know anything about television in general and about drama in particular, but even with my scant expertise I reckoned that shooting a cop-show must involve people with cameras, or maybe some lights, or something. I looked again at the unfolding scene and no-one seemed to be stepping forward to shout 'cut'. The long and the short of it was that the Head of News and I were witnessing an armed robbery on the van delivering the wages, and neither of us had lifted a finger to raise the alarm or to do anything about it.

I didn't tell anyone about this little oversight, and the small unspoken hold that I therefore had over the Head of News stood me in good stead, with the result that I was attached to the BBC2 team, rather than the BBC1 team. The reason why this was good is that the Duty Editor of the BBC1 team was a dyed in the wool hard-arse who detested Graduate Trainees because he thought they were over-privileged little snots who shouldn't be in the newsroom for at least another five years. The Duty Editor of BBC2, however, was an excellent bloke from New Zealand who believed in giving us a break and some actual work to do. Therefore while my mates who were attached to BBC1 were told to sit there, watch what was happening, and shut the hell up, I was given a whole range of tasks to do. All of them were menial, of course, but that didn't matter.

I was working on the BBC News and that was thrill enough.

I remember my first sight of Richard Baker, who was then a legendary figure who had read the news for many years. Like most people on the telly, he was far smaller than I had expected him to be. Also Richard Whitmore, younger and rather more suave. Then there was the very scary Angela Rippon – still in her pre Morecambe and Wise days when no-one yet knew that she had a sense of humour. I vividly recall that actually seeing these household names in the flesh was intensely exciting. These were the people who appeared on the telly for heaven's sake. Reading the news. My Mum and Dad watched them every night, and here they were for real.

In those days you had to write news stories one paragraph at a time, and each paragraph was typed onto its own half-sheet of paper. Every page had the slug-line of the story on the top left of the paper, and the name of the sub-editor responsible for writing it on the top right.

So the very first time I actually got to be responsible for writing one of these stories was on the lunchtime bulletin. The story was a very brief update on the developing situation in what by then was Zimbabwe. The entire script was only about three paragraphs long, and the slug-line was on the top left and my name was on the top right.

I spent most of the morning writing and re-writing and then re-writing again this little story, so many times in fact that in the end I couldn't even work out if it made sense or not. But these were my words, words written by me, which were going to be read out on the television to the waiting world – by Angela Rippon!

Eventually, after more revisions than the Good Friday Agreement, I was forced to hand my story in and I watched it being collated with all the rest, passing through the hands of the Duty Editor, and then to the newsreader. I watched Angela

Rippon as she started to look through her stories, a page at a time. Desperate to make a good impression, I was intently monitoring the expression on her face as she leafed through the various stories, muttering them softly to herself to ensure she had got the correct sense of the sentence structure. I saw her stop when she got to the story I had written. I think my heart stopped as well. Then her eyes flickered over the title of the story, and then her eyes flickered over my by-line on the top right. Her expression was exactly the one she might have adopted if she had discovered that someone had put a turd in her sandwich. She looked up, and in her best inimitable and rather imperious voice, she demanded 'Who's Stuart Prebble?'

I froze. That would be me. Had I spelled something incorrectly? Split an infinitive? Inadvertently put the word 'fucking' in between 'the' and 'Prime Minister'? I had been in such a state that anything was possible.

Sitting next to her, the kindly Duty Editor from New Zealand pointed me out. Her expression did not change, as she asked me her question. 'How do you pronounce Ndabaningi Sithole?' She might have asked me to unlock the timeless mystery of the hidden runes in the Great Pyramid of Giza. Naturally I didn't have a clue and she looked back at the Duty Editor as if in despair at the primordial idiocy of the people who surrounded her. That was the day I learned about the BBC Pronunciations Unit, and Angela's pronunciation of Ndabaningi Sithole eventually became something to be celebrated; a thing of legend.

The only other anecdote I'm going to share from those happy days was from the time I was on a three-month attachment to Radio Stoke. I was staying in a guest house run by a very kindly woman called Mrs Rose, and sharing a room with a plumber who had left his wife and used to bring all manner of dreadful old boilers back to the room for a quickie when he thought I was asleep. Oh happy days.

Anyway, the News Editor at the time was a marvellous bloke called Terry Berkeley, who was another one who had come up the hard way, but who believed in giving News Trainees a chance. Every day, around about 10.30 a.m., the DJ who was running the morning show would hand over to the newsroom where the News Editor would update the listeners on the stories the news-team was preparing for the main bulletin coming up at lunchtime. Terry didn't need a script, and used to more or less make this up as he went along. I was always especially impressed when he ended his round-up of unfolding stories with the weather forecast. We had no weather forecast from the Met Office at that time of day, so Terry used to glance out of the window, look up at the sky and, without hesitating for a second, say something like '… and the weather? Dry with some sunny periods. Chance of a light shower about 4 p.m., but very little chance of a frost overnight.' I swear that Terry's summary based on a glance at the sky was every bit as accurate as the one from the Met Office.

So to come to the point, there were two cub reporters on attachment to the station at the time. There was me, who lived locally with Mrs Rose and the conscientious plumber who brought his work home, and there was a bloke called Rob Elliott who used to have to travel up to Stoke from Birmingham every day. On this particular morning the big story was that there was black ice and fog on the motorway and Terry was giving a live update via the microphone on his desk in the newsroom when Rob walked through the door.

Without missing a beat, Terry Berkeley said, 'and as I speak I see that our roving reporter Rob Elliot has just arrived in the newsroom.' At this point Rob started to wave his arms about and was frantically mouthing 'no, no', but by this time Terry was on an unstoppable roll. 'Rob has been out and about this morning on the motorway on his way up from Birmingham, speaking to motorists and the emergency services, and is here with an on-the-spot eyewitness report.' He shoved the microphone towards Rob, who stopped waving and mouthing and started talking.

'Well Terry, visibility on the motorway is down to about fifty yards in places, there is freezing fog and black ice on the roads, and there have been a number of accidents. There are hold-ups in all three lanes of the motorway and the hard shoulder is also blocked, preventing access for emergency vehicles carrying casualties. The police have given a special warning about motorists driving too close to each other.' Now his tone turned grave. 'The message from the police and emergency services is, please keep your distance.'

With that, the news-insert ended and Terry signed off and returned the listeners to the care of the studio downstairs.

'That was great,' he said to Rob, 'but what was all that waving your arms about for?'

'I got pissed last night and slept under the desk in the studio,' said Rob, and walked out to take his morning shower.

The Backward Ghoster

oes anyone remember trade unions?

Blimey. All that seems like a long time ago, doesn't it?

I was going through some archive film recently for a TV series we were making about Tony Blair and I came across an interview with Arthur Scargill from around about 1995. Strange-looking bloke with a very dodgy haircut but, even after having been totally trounced by Mrs Thatcher, he still had a wild look in his eyes when he was accusing Tony Blair of 'a declaration of war against the trade union movement'. At the same TUC conference the leader of the then mighty Transport and General Workers' Union Bill Morris was interviewed saying that they didn't want to dominate new Labour; all they were asking for was 'a partnership of equals'.

And only a dozen years ago! Whatever happened to all that?

Grumpy Old Men are grumpy about trade unions because they're another thing from our youth that got all messed up. I remember having to join NALGO when I worked briefly in Lewisham Library and thinking that it was a good thing for the staff and workers to have some representation of their common interest. Heaven knows the management was tyrannical enough as it was; you could only guess what it would have been like without the modest efforts of the one employee who was also the union rep and who therefore didn't have to be terrified of losing his job (other, of course, than any friend of the Town Clerk).

Then when I was at university up in the north-east we used to go to the Durham Miners Gala. Colliery brass bands from pits all around the region would collect in Durham for an annual picnic in July. They used to call it 'the big meeting' and they had been doing so every year since 1872. Bloody thousands of them and their families, all marching into town, their emblems hoisted over their heads.

These banners were made of silk and held up proudly in front of the contingent from every colliery. They had vivid and evocative images embroidered on the front. Of the winding wheel at the pithead, or of a local bridge or river, or of respected figures from the history of the village they came from. Some were ostensibly political – like Chopwell, locally known as 'Little Moscow', which had pictures of Marx, though for all the genuine politicisation of the average miner in those days it might as well have been Groucho.

Below the images they bore slogans which seemed brave and feisty, but which now seem sad and even quaint. Stuff like 'Socialism through evolution' or 'Need before greed'. See what I mean?

In those days the trade unions were repositories of tradition, of pride in the skills and crafts of their members, and of honest work honestly done. There was a belief in justice and some kind of fairness in the distribution of the wealth generated by their labour. Men like Jack Jones and Hugh Scanlon – anyone remember them? Giant figures. Respected men. I remember avoiding going to Spain for about ten years after I heard Jack Jones say that you shouldn't go there for your holidays. These were people with high moral principles that you could look up to.

Whatever happened to all that, eh? Where are they now? The successors of these great men in the wider trade union movement

are boring, irrelevant, mostly mean-spirited and nasty little bastards. Which makes some of us Grumpy. It's easy to blame Mrs Thatcher and Tony Blair for the demise of the trade unions, and many of us do, but if we are completely honest we have to admit that it was mostly their own fault.

My first real experience of trade unionism was when I was a BBC journalist trainee and I was given a film to cut for the BBC News at lunchtime. It's hard to convey how exhilarating it was for me to be given the actual responsibility to actually edit a piece of actual film which would actually go on the actual telly. It was a report by a bloke called Stephen Darling and was from Cyprus where people were shooting at each other. I remember the film editor winding the 16mm celluloid film in between all the cogs and sprockets onto this old Steenbeck, which seemed so ancient it was practically steam-driven, and watching as the images flickered to life on a tiny screen at the back.

The cameraman was perched behind a barricade manned by two fighters with guns. A couple of shots rang out, smoke filled the air, one of the fighters leapt up and ran across a square, and Stephen Darling popped up in front of them and began his 'piece to camera'. 'Here on the front line of the brutal conflict between two armed gangs …' Intrepid stuff, I thought, but then Stephen fluffed his words and the camera stopped rolling. Take 2. The cameraman was crouched in position, two shots rang out, smoke filled the air, and one of the fighters ran across the square. Stephen Darling popped up and did his piece to camera.

There we are, another childhood illusion shattered. However, that's not the point of the story. The point of the story is that within a couple of minutes of starting this exercise I noticed that the film editor had stopped working. He had put down the pieces of film and was sitting back in his chair. I waited for a few minutes, wondering what was happening, and assuming that maybe he was thinking. After a while my curiosity overcame me and I asked him why we had stopped. At first he didn't say anything, but just pointed to my elbow, which was resting on the corner of the editing machine.

'You're touching the Steenbeck,' he said.

Still a bit confused, I took my elbow off of the machine and the editor resumed his work. Only later did I learn that members of his union would not allow members of my union to touch their editing equipment.

What he didn't know was that, later that evening after everyone else had gone home, I popped back to the editing suite, slipped off my trousers and sat on his editing machine for a couple of minutes with my bare arse.

Of course television was as rife with appalling bad practices as were the print unions, which were more notorious, and truly it was a bloody scandal.

At one time I worked on the regional news magazine programme *Granada Reports*, and if any person appearing in a story we were covering had to use an object of any kind at all, we would have to take a props man out with us as part of the film crew. I'm talking about filming a chef who might want to pick up a saucepan. Yes, along with the six-person crew – cameraman, assistant cameraman, sound man, lighting man, reporter and PA, you had to take a props man. He didn't have anything to do, nothing at all, but he had to be taken along because we were using props, and if you were using props, you had to have a props man with you.

On one occasion we were going to produce a little feature about a juggler from a visiting circus, and although we had been told that in no circumstances whatsoever would this juggler allow anyone other than himself to touch his balls, as it were, I knew we would have to send a props man. So I sent a props man with the crew and when they arrived I got a call from the reporter saying that the props man would not allow the crew to film.

'Why not?' I not unreasonably asked.

'Because he says we need another props man.'

'Why is that?'

'Because he says that the props are moving, and so therefore they count as 'action props' and for 'action props' you also need a second props man'.

'But none of them is allowed to touch the jugglers' balls anyway.' You can see how this was getting a bit bizarre.

'I know,' said the reporter, 'but apparently that's not the point.'

It wasn't. The point was that we had to send another props man out onto the shoot, and when the reporter came back with his footage, we had to bring in the commissionaire to look at the footage to give us his view on whether two props men had been enough. The commissionaire was the props men's trade union representative, and he had to decide whether to allow us to show the film on the evening news. On that occasion he was very grudging, but he did.

Yes that's right. The commissionaire decided what was on the evening news.

Worst of all were the electricians. They were bloody notorious for demanding to be taken on location, even when there were no lights needed and even when there was no chance whatsoever that a light would be needed. When I worked on *World in Action*, we quite often wanted to get some footage at one of the party conferences in Blackpool or Brighton, but we never could. The reason? Because we couldn't afford to send the minimum of three electricians by plane to Brighton to notionally light a huge hall which had already been lit.

I'm not joking. Because it would have taken no fewer than three electricians to light a hall the size of the conference centre, the electricians' union demanded that three electricians would be sent, even though the hall had been pre-lit – by other members of the electricians' union. There were very few things of this kind that the Granada management drew the line at, but this was one of them, the result of which was that a major ITV network current affairs programme could never obtain footage of the political party conferences. Literally keeping viewers in the dark.

Were we therefore allowed to buy in the footage from ITN or another source? Of course not, because the unions wouldn't allow us to buy in material that we could in theory have shot for ourselves. Does anyone believe this?

There were endless stories about the rule regarding the ten-hour break, which said that if for any reason the technical crew had less than ten hours off between ending work and starting work, all work done in that second shift would have to be paid at double-time. For the sake of any very young reader who may have slipped through the net, that means double the normal rate of pay. So if that second shift lasted ten hours, the person working them would be paid for twenty hours of work. If the same thing happened again, the rate of pay for the next day would be doubled again, so that the person working them was earning four times their usual hourly rate. And so on.

Naturally we were all under the very strictest instructions from the management not ever to allow the crew to break the ten-hour break, but occasionally, due to late planes and trains combined with unmovable deadlines, it was unavoidable.

My favourite story about the ten-hour break is told by my mate Ian McBride who was on a crash-bang-wallop fast shoot in America, trying to finish a film in a few days and get it back to England for a speedy edit and transmission on the following Monday. He and the researcher had been tearing their hair out, staying up late at night, fixing interviewees for the following day, doing the journalism and writing the scripts on the run. In the course of all this mayhem they had to make travel arrangements for eight people because the technical crew consisted of a cameraman, an assistant cameraman, a sound man, an assistant sound man, an electrician, and a production assistant, as well as the producer and researcher. Running as quickly as possible against a fast-ticking clock, they had crossed backwards and forwards over several time zones, which meant that though they had not actually ever had less than a ten-hour break between working shifts, the clock said that they had.

Ian's story recalls how the electrician had not erected or switched on a single light since he had left England. Indeed, I think maybe had not even brought any lights with him. One evening, Ian was rushing from one room to the next, trying to sort out the next day of filming, when he spotted the electrician doing the back-stroke down the length of the hotel pool. The sparks, who was called Tommy (all sparks are called Tommy), called Ian over and said, 'Hoy Ian, you do know that we've broken the ten-hour break, don't you?' all the while never interrupting his stroke.

What do you reckon?

So to come to the title of the chapter, the backward ghoster. A wonderful expression, I think you'll agree. I can't remember the exact rule, but I think it was something like this. If the technical crew broke the ten-hour break, and then didn't get another break with time for a three-course meal and a personal massage in it, or something, this would initiate the 'backward ghoster'. This meant that not only were current hours worked being paid at multiple rates of pay, but that previous hours worked, which had originally been paid at normal time, would now be paid at multiple rates of pay also. So I think the all-time record was taken by a crew which had been filming across several time zones in Africa, and had no doubt been working very hard, but were being paid sixteen times their usual rate of pay.

When you hear this, you sort of know that something had to give.

But it's a pity, because in the course of taking the piss in this way, these morons ended up making the trade unions totally powerless, so that now the pendulum has swung to almost the complete opposite extreme and we have no realistic limits to the numbers of hours anyone can be forced to work. We have executives being paid absolutely breathtaking and egregious multiples of the salaries being paid to their workers because no-one has the guts or power to do anything about it. And we have cocklepickers being drowned on beaches thousands of miles from their homes.

Which is, as they say, 'not cool'. And makes us Grumpy.

Role Models

So now that you have got a job, done your probation, hopefully not irritated too many people, ignored the manuals, how are you going to prosper?

Well, the answer may well be to look for a suitable role model – someone who impresses you and seems to have made a go of it, and try to do what they do. However, a worrying trend, so far as Grumpies and up-and-coming Grumpies are concerned, is the growing fashion there seems to be for bosses to be bloody rude to their employees. That's because Grumpies aren't very good at handling people who are rude to us. We have this terrible tendency to respond badly to provocation or irritation, which can seriously shorten a career.

As with so much else that is wrong with the world these days, I blame the telly. In recent years the telly has been responsible for celebrating ignorance (*Big Brother*), for celebrating humiliation (*I'm a Celebrity*), and for celebrating greed (just about everything). More recently it has taken to celebrating rudeness and bullying with a whole collection of programmes about various aspects of business. Time was when the perceived wisdom among TV people was that the whole world of business didn't really work. *The Money Programme* was about as exciting as it got – a series which everyone respected but which no-one watched.

I think the first foray into this area that I remember involved the genial old buffer John Harvey-Jones, whom I seem to recall used to be the boss at ICI when it was thought to be a good company. If I remember correctly he ran around the place looking at other people's businesses and, from time to time, we were a bit shocked that he was occasionally less than totally complimentary to the people running them. However, his purpose was basically constructive and his manner was always genial. Certainly he never swore at anyone.

I may have got this mixed up, but I think this mantle passed to Sir Gerry Robinson, a former boss of mine and current Grumpy Old Man of this parish. Gerry has turned a twinkle in the eye into an art form, and simple old-style charm has taken him further than it has taken anyone I have ever met. I think the old-fashioned expression is something like 'he could charm the wallpaper off the walls' but it's actually true that Gerry could fire someone and make them feel grateful to him for doing so. Gerry, of course, didn't believe that his success depended on his charm. He believed that it depended on his ability to make everything so simple. For example, he once told me that his job was ever so easy.

'I just say 'I want another 20%,' and then you say 'but Gerry we gave you an extra 20% last year and the year before, and there just aren't any more 20%s to be had', and I wait until you've finished and then I say, 'but I want another 20%' and in the end you'll get me the extra 20%, and if you don't, I'll find someone who will.' And then he smiled. 'See? Simple.' That's why Gerry used to be able to go home early – on the three days per week he worked. It was all so simple.

I particularly loved Gerry's recent series on the BBC about the problems in the NHS. He spent weeks looking into the detailed running of a big major hospital and came up with a very simple solution, which was basically that 'everyone has to work harder', but he did it in such a nice way that all the people left having to work harder were grateful to him. A class act, if ever I saw one.

However, it's all down-hill from there. The first in the new wave of looking at work and business was probably *Dragon's Den*. The original theme was that ordinary people with a decent business idea but no clue how to implement it would come and get some investment and advice from four people who had made it big in business themselves. The twist was that these 'dragons' would be investing their own money, which was good, because it gave what the broadcasters now call 'a bit of jeopardy' on both sides.

The shortcoming of the series was that you didn't know anything about the would-be entrepreneurs before or after their encounter, but that was alright. If I remember, series one was quite watchable, sometimes entertaining, and contained a mix of fairly decent ideas with some no-hopers, but unless my memory deceives me, no-one was humiliated.

However, one of the unpleasant things about the media in general and the telly in particular is that, year by year, everything has to be pushed just a bit further. The show may have a new editor who won't be able to make a name for him- or herself if they leave well enough alone, so they push the producers just a bit closer to the edge. Or suddenly maybe there is another show on another channel which is doing basically the same thing as your show is doing, but has added a twist of cruelty or insult or humiliation. Or something.

The result is that a show which was in reasonable taste this year will be in suspect taste next year and has to be in bad taste the year after. A series which had an element of cruelty this year has to be feeding people to the lions next year, and so on. And thus it has been with *Dragon's Den*, on which every season the 'dragons' have become more smug, vile and gratuitously rude, and the contestants have become more hapless, pathetic, idiotic and therefore degraded.

I should quickly add before going any further that, like most Grumpies, I prefer prejudice to facts, and of course like many people who complain I haven't actually seen very much of the programmes I criticise with such conviction and authority. The day that we Grumpies have actually to have seen a programme in order to feel qualified to complain about it would be a sad day indeed. However, where once (I think) a contestant on *Dragon's Den* without a clue would be listened to, perhaps in dumb-struck silence, but mercifully briefly – nowadays their plight is strung out, their spit-roasting more fiery, their humiliation more complete. Where once the Dragons would content themselves with dismissing an idea with, at worst, some evident impatience, nowadays they have to show how very clever they are by forensically unravelling the person and their idea on camera.

They all want to be Simon Cowell and make a name for themselves by being brutal. One of them – is it the bloke who owns the football team? – has obviously been rehearsing what he thinks are his colourful lines, and is always waiting for the opportunity to trot them out. Ideally the contestant will be visibly upset so that we can zoom in on their face and therefore enjoy their discomfort all the more.

These programmes make me sick.

Even worse than *Dragon's Den*, is the phenomenon of *The Apprentice*, in which we are apparently searching for someone who wants to earn '£100,000 a year' working as an assistant to Sir Alan Sugar. We'll come to everything that is irritating about Alan Sugar in a moment, but just think for a minute about the people who appear to want to work for him.

I know from personal experience that if a CEO of a decent-sized business with a good reputation advertises for an Executive Assistant, especially with a six-figure salary, the response is going to be extraordinary. I've done exactly this three or four times in recent years and I have to tell you that the calibre of the applicants takes your breath away. Dazzling women (for mostly they are) who have a great degree from a great university, have gone on to do an MBA, often have travelled widely, may well speak several languages, and exhibit a wisdom which totally belies their still young age. Smart, classy and impressive. Someone, somewhere, is cloning them, because there are a lot of them and they are a knock-out.

Meanwhile in *The Apprentice* we are constantly being told about the many thousands of applicants have been short-listed to get to the sixteen people who are going to appear on this show. So with all those terrific young people out there, how can it be possible that we end up with so many nasty, back-stabbing, thick, rude, prejudiced, unprepossessing people? Does this just tell us that you've got to be a sub-standard person to want to appear in a reality show? Maybe. Probably the kind of people I'm talking about would simply be far too sensible to want to appear on a reality show, or to be willing to put up with Sir Alan Sugar for five seconds, let alone a year. But I think it is more likely to be something else.

More probably it tells us that the producers think it would not be anywhere near so entertaining to see a competition among the genuinely talented, and I think they are probably right. Impressive people with brains, qualifications, good manners and a bit of integrity would be unlikely to be willing to engage in a programme which is structured at every stage so that you are obliged to stab your colleagues in the back, and then in the front, and then befriend them again, and then stab them all over again next week.

Instead, what we apparently want to see is a competition among a bunch of egotistical, not very bright, selfish air-heads, very few of whom have achieved a thing worth achieving in their whole lives. The 'I'm a very special person' mentality which imbues all those complete wankers who compete in *The X Factor* and its many variations, is writ large in these people, in addition to which they are occasionally vile and vindictive.

Which may be no problem if these shows were purely for escapist entertainment, but they aren't. The fact is that ordinary people watch these shows, and think that this must be the way to get on in business.

This is where the young and aspiring entrepreneurs are getting their tuition about what it takes to succeed in business. Apparently you have to be an uncouth, ill-mannered, bad-tempered, ill-tutored lout in order to get on. There was one guy in the recent series of *The Apprentice* – I think his name was Lohit or something, who was dismissed with something near total contempt because he had committed the cardinal sin of being 'a nice guy'. Sure he was a bit of a lettuce, but I'd rather have had him working for me than any of the other toss-pots who fared so much better.

And what about the knight himself? The whole premise of the show is that Sir Alan Sugar is a self-made man of the kind we would all aspire to be. He's seen in his private jet, we see shots of impressive buildings which we're supposed to assume he owns, and several gadgets made by his companies mysteriously appear in shot. I believe they call this 'product placement' and it's against the broadcasting regulations, but that's not what we're writing about here.

Sir Alan is the 'hero' to all of the aspiring apprentices and, presumably, to us too. But what is he? He is a rude, shrewd bully, who shouts people down, humiliates them in front of colleagues, and most of the time seems to enjoy the power that goes with being able to jab your finger at someone who can't answer back and say 'you're fired'. And the joy of firing someone in public is so great, apparently, that it's become the catchphrase of the show – like firing someone is a piece of entertainment – which it quite literally is in this programme.

So this show is utterly nauseating but, as you can probably tell, even though it makes me want to take a shower afterwards to clean away the slime, it's a show I have occasionally found myself watching. However, nothing could persuade me to sit through an episode of anything involving Gordon Ramsay.

Can anyone explain to me how this bloke doesn't get himself punched into the middle of next week? All joking aside, I just don't get it. I'm not a violent person myself, but I know that I wouldn't be able to put up with more than about fifteen seconds of the kind of shit he thinks it's OK to unleash, without ripping his bloody stupid head off and taking a shit in it. He's the most rude, abusive, aggressive, bad tempered, bullying bastard I've ever seen on the television, and yet it seems that the public loves him. How can that be OK? And what does it say about us that we are not only willing to stand by and watch him take advantage of a load of hapless twots who know no better than to put themselves up for it, but we actually seem to enjoy it?

Eh?

So now, the dilemma for the Grumpy Old Man, or indeed for his apprentice, is what to do if you find yourself working in a company where the boss has been watching too much reality TV and thinks he wants to be macho man. In other words, what do you do if the person you report to is a supercilious arse-head who thinks it's OK to treat you like shit?

Well that's a tricky one, and in my thirty years working in big organisations, where you can't necessarily choose your colleagues or superiors, I can't honestly say that it's one I ever really got right. However, this is where Grumpy Old Men-dom can come in handy. This is where the syndrome that is Grumpiness can genuinely help. And lord preserve us, despite our earlier declaration and our best intentions, it seems that we're writing a self-help book after all. Would you believe it?

I've said before that Grumpiness is not about being miserable or unhappy. It's not about being depressed or grumpy. Grumpiness as we have re-defined it is just a way of looking at the world. Where everyone else is seeing advertising, Grumpies are seeing bullshit. Where everyone else is seeing Members of Parliament, Grumpies are seeing egotistical little toads croaking at the moon. Where everyone else seems to be seeing progress, we're seeing an apparently relentless flight towards a world it's impossible for civilised human beings to live in.

So when everyone else at your place of work may be seeing an intimidating and foul-mouthed bully, Grumpies are just seeing a little wanker. And if you are among the former category and have someone like this to deal with in your place of work, we recommend that you adopt some of the attitudes and prejudices of the Grumpy, and get a whole new perspective on the problem.

Let's take Alan Sugar as an example. We're not being unkind to do so because, in adopting the persona he has in *The Apprentice*, he's clearly embracing and glorying in all the traits I'm about to identify. As we said earlier, the whole premise of the series is that this is someone who is successful, has made a shit-load of money, has a lifestyle we would all love to emulate, and is at the apogee of success as it is defined in the 21st century. Most viewers are seeing a modern-day hero who, sure, has had to have a strong personality to achieve what he has achieved, but that's business. That's what most people are seeing.

What Grumpies are seeing, by contrast, is an odd little character out of Middle Earth who has spent too long too far away from The Shire. We're seeing a strange little bloke who is compensating for being a runt by also being a bully. When Alan Sugar says in the introduction to the series 'no-one is going to make a fool out of me', Grumpies are all thinking that no-one needs to, because you've managed to do that so well yourself. No-one *could* make more of a fool of you than you have managed without our help.

We're all supposed to admire Sir Alan Sugar because he's a self-made man, which may be so, but I know quite a few self-made men who have found it possible to succeed without reminding everyone at every opportunity that they did so. Self-made men who don't have to prove apparently every minute of every day that they are a success and that you are 'a shambles' or whatever was the nasty adjective which became so beloved by the producers that they used it weekly in the headlines.

So if you have got a budding Alan Sugar for a boss, and everyone around you is seeing someone to be afraid of, or intimidated by, we recommend that you adopt the perspective adopted by all Grumpies everywhere, and instead see a pathetic bore with a complex of some sort that he's trying to work himself out of. Don't get caught up in his little psychosis. Be in contempt and rise above it, and if you can't, choose the right moment and tell him to go take a walk into a wall. Sure you'll lose your job, but it'll be a good anecdote you'll be proud to tell for the rest of your life.

McJobs

I heard a story on the radio this morning about a campaign to persuade the *Oxford English Dictionary* to change their printed definition of the word 'McJobs'. Is this idea utterly priceless, or what?

It seems that this little jaunt was dreamed up by McDonalds themselves who are irritated, no doubt understandably, that their brand has been hi-jacked and used as a prefix to denote anything that is unsubstantial, plastic, or generally naff. My favourite use or abuse of their highly prized prefix is in the delightful term 'McMansions' to denote the kinds of houses that first-division footballers live in. It's a perfect description. When you say the word 'McMansions', we all have precisely the same picture in our mind's eye. You know, Doric columns, statues in the garden, unwise indoor fountains, dodgy mirrors and even dodgier pictures, etc.

Anyway, as everybody knows, the term McJobs has long been used as a term to describe any utterly pointless work where the employees have no motivation, no training, no prospects and quite often speak no English. Once again, you can just take a look at the vacant expressions on the faces of so many of the people who work in these hell-holes, and they speak for themselves with far more eloquence than any mere poet could contrive.

So it seems that the word McJobs has gone into the *Oxford English Dictionary* with some definition that summarises this syndrome, and the McDonalds people want to get it changed.

Nothing too weird about that, you might suppose, because commercial companies will always talk whatever bollocks is necessary to protect their business; that's what business people do. But here is the weird thing. Some total drong of a backbench MP has come out in support of this asinine idea, and has even tabled an early-day motion (which is the Parliamentary equivalent of a sandwich board but with less effect) deploring this definition and asking for a new one.

Obviously he has already achieved his main objective which is to get his idiot self on the radio, but now having done so, he's coming out with all this total and unutterable bollocks about how the term is disrespectful to the many thousands of decent hard-working people who work in McDonalds and other similar 'restaurants'. (It's me putting speech marks around 'restaurants' by the way, not him – he was on the radio so I couldn't see if he was putting up two pairs of two fingers in that irritating way that I believe denotes them.) He was going on and on about 'some of my most hard-working constituents' and about 'very good people who have come here from other countries, seeking honest work and a way of improving themselves'.

All this went on for what seemed like ten minutes but was probably three, and then they had the bloke from the *OED* on the line to defend the point of view of the dictionary (and think how weird it must be to be the spokesman on behalf of all words).

Obviously I don't know what age this bloke can have been, but what I do know about him for sure is that he cannot have been one of us. No chance at all that he was a Grumpy Old Man. I know this because if he had been a Grumpy Old Man he would have been unable to prevent himself from bursting out laughing, and pointing out that, by and large, dictionaries indicate what words *do* mean, rather than what some self-important gunk-head would *like* them to mean. Instead of this, he managed to remain polite and restrained, and confined himself to indicating that he had before him about twenty-five pages of examples of the word being used in the context that is outlined in the dictionary definition, and that it would only be appropriate for the *OED* to change the definition if people started using the word with the meaning that the MP had in mind.

Most people would have been devastated and would have crawled off into their shells, but this bloke was a backbench MP with oatmeal where his brain should have been, so of course he declined to concede the point and went on and on and on.

It's not particularly relevant to anything, but I ask you. Really. How could anybody be anything other than Grumpy when these are the sort of people we are electing to represent us? No really.

Meetings

What on earth do people find to do for all these hours that they spend in the office? To get a clue, try telephoning any person in any business at any time of the day and ask if you can be put through to them. I'll bet the chances are that the secretary or PA will say 'he's in a meeting'; and the chances are that she (if it's a she) will speak the words as though it's the equivalent of 'he's at prayer'. He's in a meeting and therefore 'cannot be disturbed'.

No-one who hasn't worked in a big corporation can ever work out how it can be possible that so many people spend so much time in so many meetings. What can they all find to talk about? Why doesn't someone just decide something, so they can all get on with it?

So what does this mean, 'in a meeting'?, and what is it about all these meetings that no-one can be disturbed when they are in them? Are they having sex? Not usually. Are they discussing secrets? Very seldom. What is so sacrosanct about 'meetings' and why do there seem to be so many of them?

Well there are many awful and depressing things about working for a big corporation, and heaven knows we're covering many of them in this small volume. However, I think we can honestly say that the worst thing about it – the thing that makes Grumpy

Old Men and Women the most grumpy of all – is all the stupid bloody meetings.

Meetings meetings meetings meeting meetings. Meetings to discuss other meetings. Meetings to recommend things to more important meetings. Meetings to coordinate the activities of other meetings. Meetings to keep people informed of what is going on in lesser meetings. Meetings that, when you get there, nobody seems to know what they are supposed to achieve. All totally bloody pointless other than to perpetuate all the bollocks and to make largely useless and dysfunctional people feel important.

When I worked as a suit in ITV, the week very often consisted entirely of meetings. Nothing else. One after the other, end to end. Any time not spent in meetings was spent on the way to or from meetings. The whole day would be devoted to them. Not a minute to breathe or to think or to take a shit. Which is probably why so many people in business have that rather stressed and uncomfortable expression permanently on their faces.

The early days

When you first start attending business meetings as one of the juniors on the team, you're completely self-conscious and totally preoccupied with the idea of not making a tit of yourself. Obviously the main reason that you've wanted to come to this or any meeting is that you want the chance to impress the boss, so you find yourself wondering about all sorts of things that would never occur to someone less shallow than you are.

For example, there is the question of the tea. A tricky one, this. Usually there is a main table with chairs around for the meeting, and a side-table with tea, coffee and water on it where people help themselves. Do you make your own tea and ask the boss if you can get one for him, or don't you? If you don't, chances are he's going to think you are a rude little bugger with no respect for your elders or betters. If you do, he's going to think you are a little creep who plans to climb the greasy pole by sucking up to seniors rather than doing anything actually useful. It's all rather difficult, isn't it?

Then there is the question of where you should sit.

Obviously the boss is going to sit at the top of the table, so do you show that you are not intimidated by sitting next to him? On the one hand that could be disastrous because he might say 'not there, Twaddle, obviously I need the FD to sit next to me' in which case you're humiliated and by then all the other seats are taken. Or on the other hand he might be impressed that you are not over-awed by his magnificence and make a mental note that 'this bloke is going places'.

Of course, it's only when you get to be the boss yourself that you realise that actually he doesn't take a blind bit of notice of you, nor could he give a monkey's arse where you sit, because you are totally irrelevant. In the unlikely event that he gives you a second thought at all, he's most likely to be thinking 'who invited this little prat to my meeting?'

Once the meeting is under way, you marvel at how relaxed everyone else seems to be, and wonder how on earth they manage to seem so at ease and to sound so articulate. You try hard to follow the discussion, and you are constantly formulating in your head what might be your next contribution, but all the time you are anxious about what would happen if, out of the blue, the Chairman suddenly turned to you and asked you what you thought about what was going on.

It's like you are back at school and in the classroom of your scariest teacher who might throw a board rubber at you at any moment he thinks you aren't paying attention. 'Christ, what would I say if someone asked me a question now?'

Once you start to think like this, it's a short road to disaster. No sooner have you formulated a reasonably intelligent thing to say about the subject currently under debate than the discussion has moved on, and the thing you've intended to say is irrelevant. Worse than that, if you were forced to say it, you'd be commenting on something that was discussed several minutes ago, making you look like a retard. You have to abandon the thing you have in your mind, and focus anew on the next stage of the discussion, ready at any time with something worthwhile to say if called upon unexpectedly.

Then, horror of horrors, you realise that the meeting is coming to a close, and you haven't said anything at all. The others are inevitably going to conclude that you are a lightweight. You wait for a quiet moment just before the end and give your little summary of everything you've mentally recorded in the past hour. You hope that perhaps you'll sound like a wise person, able to see the big picture, maybe sort of summing up the discussion. What you actually sound like is someone who took all this time to understand what everyone else had understood as the meeting went along, and has only just got up to speed.

'Thank you Dawdle,' says the Chairman. 'I'm sure that was very helpful for anyone who missed the discussion.' And now you wish you were dead. As indeed, so far as he is concerned, you are.

Accumulating meetings

There are very few things in life that are universally true, but one rare exception is the fact that everyone always thinks that the meeting they are not in is the interesting one. Do you know what I mean? No matter how much of your week is taken up with one endless and pointless meeting after another, you always think that the meeting you are not invited to is the one that makes all the interesting decisions.

That's the meeting in the office with the glass walls, so that you can see all the people on the next rung up the ladder to you laughing and pouring themselves a glass of orange juice and grabbing an all-butter croissant before they get down to business. It's the one that the MD attends, and so everyone there gets the chance to show off. It's the one where they have access to the confidential papers which are not available to people at your level of the business. The one at which they close the Venetian blinds when someone is doing a presentation. The one where they collect the papers at the end and take them to the shredder.

That's the meeting you want to be in.

And every time you get a little step further up the career ladder, and find yourself in the meeting you thought you always wanted to be in, you inevitably find that this is still not the meeting at which the key decisions are taken. No, what you find is that this meeting is the one that does all the hard work of sifting through the options, the one where everyone attending has to have done some serious reading the night before. This meeting may even be the one that has the power to make a recommendation to the next meeting, but it's the next meeting that you really want to go to. And if and when you ever get to be invited to that next meeting, you find that that's not the key meeting either.

So the problem is that as you go through your career you accumulate new meetings as you gain seniority. But that's alright, because as you start going to the more important meetings obviously you stop going to some of the less important meetings. Right? Of course not. Why not?

Because when you were first invited to the less important meeting, you were one of the most junior people at the meeting. You took a long time to get the measure of the meeting and were initially timid in making your contributions. Other more senior people took control, made all the important points, and drove the thing to its conclusion. You were made to feel small and insignificant. Sometimes you might pluck up courage to say something, and everyone else would look at each other as if to ask who had invited the village idiot by mistake.

With the passage of enough time, you will probably find that you have become that more powerful person at the meeting whom others are trying to impress. You are the one who gets to intimidate some of the fresh new faces who are joining the meeting for the first time. Having waited all this time, and having had others lording it over you for so long, the last thing you want to do is to absent yourself and only attend more important meetings at which you are once again the most junior person present. And boy are you going to enjoy it. What you probably are not going to do is to stop coming to this meeting altogether, which means that you will accumulate more and more meetings, and so your life will be full of meaningless shit.

Before long you may find that other aspects of your life will be run as though you were in a business meeting.

At the family dinner table, you'll find yourself organising the conversation, and at the end of what has been a chat about some domestic matter you'll find yourself saying 'So what have we decided then?' and your partner or kids will look at you and say 'You're not at work now Dad'. Has that happened to you? No? Maybe just me then.

Much worse than all that, you may well find that you have started to talk in that appalling management-speak which has polluted our language and makes most of us with a surviving brain-cell want to reach for the sick-bucket. You've heard all that stuff – 'blue-sky thinking' which means you are an air-head without a cloud to clutter up your horizon. 'Thinking outside the box' which means no-one has had a decent thought inside the box, so let's see if we can have one by getting outside of it.

There's 'pushing the envelope' which is a weird one. I think I probably can work out what 'the box' is, but what is 'the envelope' and what reason would we have to push it? I've also heard of people 'running an idea up the flagpole to see who salutes it' and seeing if an idea 'floats my boat'. For heaven's sake.

The average day

The average day for me when I was CEO of ITV often started with a 'breakfast meeting' because obviously there weren't enough hours between nine in the morning and seven in the evening to get through all the meetings I had to attend. So sometimes it made sense to steal a march on the day (whatever that means) and make an early start. Except that this meant that I had to get out of bed at six o'bloody clock at the latest if I was to have any chance of getting there on time.

The good news is that you leave home so early in the morning you might miss the worst part of the traffic; the bad news is that you have to be relatively alert at a time of the day when you are inevitably feeling like a dog's leftover elevenses.

Superficially, if you don't know any better, the idea of a breakfast meeting might seem to be relatively appealing. The chance

to have someone else cook your brekker in some nice hotel at the expense of the company. A chance to start the day with a leisurely meal under a bit less pressure than is usually the case in the office. Needless to say, the reality seldom resembles that in any way at all.

First, there is the whole question of the person you're meeting at breakfast.

In my case, my breakfast companion was usually some fat pompous prick from out of town who had taken the opportunity of a night in London to do something very unwise and usually rather sordid, and so the chance to watch him trying to use soggy fried bread as a sort of blotting paper for alcohol was not a great way to start the day. The first half of the meeting would usually be taken up by him telling me about his previous evening's adventures, often in terms more graphic than one would wish at any time of the day, let alone at breakfast.

Second, there is the matter of what to have to eat.

Usually a breakfast meeting takes place at a very expensive but still very crummy hotel, where the best it's going to be is the breakfast buffet, with everything that this implies. A big bowl of scrambled eggs of a hue that does not occur in nature and a texture which implies extrusion through an industrial process. Barely warm chipolata-style sausages, and entangled rashers of greasy streaky bacon of the kind favoured by Americans. Grilled tomatoes cooked to buggery. Cold mushrooms in grease. Ugh.

Whenever possible, I would use these occasions to have my favourite breakfast, which is a kipper. I'm fond of a kipper at almost any time, but cooking kippers in the house first thing in the morning isn't very welcome because they tend to stink out the kitchen and most of the hallway until lunchtime, which doesn't go down all that well with the family. Especially because they have to put up with the stench long after I've gone to work. So, because by and large Grumpies prefer a quiet life, ordering a kipper in a hotel seems the ideal answer.

The trouble is that eating a kipper at breakfast feels a bit like smoking a cigarette – the sort of thing you ought to ask the permission of your companion to do. Invariably they'll say that they don't mind, but very often they say they don't mind when actually they do mind, so that when it comes and is all smell and skin, you can sense them bristling. Being of the Grumpy persuasion, I usually couldn't care less about their bristling, but sometimes, if they were a marginally important business partner of some sort, their evident discomfort could demolish any last vestige of pleasure that I might otherwise have derived.

Then there are all the bones. I'm sorry to go on about this, but business breakfasts may well be an important aspect of any Grumpy's life, and while it may be that most normal people would be more concerned about something dull like what is going to be achieved at the meeting, this is the sort of thing that we are worrying about. Because it's almost impossible to eat a kipper without getting a few bones in your mouth that are too big to swallow, and so what are you supposed to do? Remember, you are in a business meeting, and already your companion is looking a bit queasy. You consider trying to swallow them anyway, but the imminent risk of getting one stuck in your throat and choking to death or making a scene which will end in your companion having to perform the Heimlich manoeuvre, seems too reckless to take.

Having reconciled yourself to the notion that these bones will have to come out, you need to spend a few minutes manoeuvring them around your mouth so that they can be made to protrude easily between your lips. Now you are aware that your guest is looking at you a bit strangely, and you wonder if he is going to be sufficiently discreet to look away at the crucial moment. You certainly don't want to be caught putting your fingers too far into your mouth and digging around for them, just at the instant that he finishes his sentence with a question. Now do you?

The only alternative to all that involves a hotel where your breakfast kipper has at some time been kept in a bag of some sort, and that's a prospect worse than imagining. So all round, a kipper during a breakfast meeting is a hazardous road, and probably is only one to travel when you reach the stage in your career when you don't give a stuff.

Anyway, despite my aversion to breakfast meetings, one way or the other I used to have to have them about two or three times a week. Once they were over, I would have to head off straight to the office where Marian, my PA, would hand me a pile of papers which I could either carry around with me all day, or loan to the janitor for something to stand on while he was changing the light bulb in the atrium. The bundle was certainly fat enough, and the latter would undoubtedly be more useful.

On top of the pile of papers would be an itinerary for the day.

9 a.m. Meeting Cable and Wireless for pointless discussion about possible areas of cooperation. (That's not exactly what it said on the piece of paper, but is a more accurate description than what it actually said.)

10 a.m. Meeting OFCOM for 116th in a series of meetings designed to sabotage the future of public service broadcasting. (Again, not exactly what the list said, but that's what it amounted to.)

11 a.m. Sales Team Routine. The regular weekly opportunity for the idiots in the sales team to explain why it was the programme planner's fault, and not their own, that nobody wanted to advertise with ITV. (This is what it said on the paper, and this is what it was.)

And so it would go on.

Every meeting would have its own agenda, and despite the fact that my PA would have included one in the pile of papers she had handed me just half an hour earlier, I always seemed to have lost it along the way. Maybe I'd doodled some notes across it. Maybe I'd cunningly fashioned it into a parachute as I fantasised about bailing out of the window. I don't know. All I know is that I never could find the agenda.

PowerPoint

Quite often these meetings will involve a presentation of some kind or other, which brings us on to the whole ghastly world of PowerPoint. I wonder how much wasted time PowerPoint is responsible for causing to fairly senior and highly paid people who would almost inevitably be better off doing almost anything else, up to and including picking their feet in Poughkeepsie*.

If you live in the world of the sane and sensible, it may even be

---

* a reference from the film *French Connection* which all true Grumpy Old Men should recognise.

that you don't know what PowerPoint is. Oh lucky lucky you. If you've ever been in a corporate meeting of any kind, you'll know only too well. So briefly, PowerPoint is a piece of kit on a computer which enables you to design a little visual aid to go along with your no doubt erudite verbal presentation. A series of slides, which can go from the very simple to the almost unbelievably elaborate, and the more and more elaborate the presentation, the more and more nerdy is the presenter. Trust me.

Whenever I realised that a presentation was going to be made with the help of PowerPoint, my heart would immediately sink.

At its most basic, the PowerPoint slide can simply repeat in written words the words the presenter is saying. In this case what the speaker has basically done is to put his notes on the screen. They'll start with the word 'Introduction', so that in case our attention has wandered off in the first couple of minutes we'll know that you are introducing your topic. Then it might say 'Background', which is helpful because who knows, you might have started telling us about your holidays in the Isle of Wight by mistake, and we'd have missed it, still thinking you were on the topic under discussion.

After a while we'll have headings like 'Options' or 'Next steps', so that what you find is that those lovely people at Microsoft have given you a whole progression from intro to conclusion, thereby taking away much of the need either to listen, or indeed to attend the meeting at all. Most often, a five-minute glance at the slides would be an effective substitute for the hour and a half you otherwise have to spend listening to it all being spelled out in exhaustive and exhausting detail.

But it's not enough for these blokes from Seattle to just give us a few tools to help us to express what was in our heads. Nothing so modest. Part of their mission is to provide a template for our lives, a substitute for all that pesky thinking, a little bit of brainwashing in favour of the gospel according to Microsoft.

For example, when you want to compose a new presentation, the PowerPoint software will ask you what sort of thing you have in mind. Are you, for example, 'communicating bad news'? If so, you click in a little box and up comes a template which suggests a whole series of slides which lay out what they see as the logical progression from 'everything's fine' to 'you're all fired'. But even then it's still not enough for these blokes to give you a series of boxes to fill in with suggested headings. They can't resist the temptation to give you a little bit of advice along the way. You're going to be treated to a little glimpse of the world according to Bill Gates, without which none of our lives can nowadays be complete. So that one of their slides is headed 'our situation' and underneath there is a little stricture saying 'state the bad news', and moreover 'be clear, don't try to obscure the situation'.

So whereas everyone else seeing this is likely to be thinking how very helpful it is for Microsoft to suggest that we don't try to obscure the situation and thanking them for the advice, the Grumpy Old Men or Women amongst us are thinking 'What the hell has it got to do with you if I want to obscure the situation?' 'Where do you people get off giving me unsolicited advice that I need to be clear about the bad news?' And being as it's me and I'm half mad and the other half paranoid, I'm starting to wonder what happens if I *do* decide to obscure the situation? Does Microsoft have a little piece of software embedded in my computer which will grass me up to Seattle? Will it wrest control of my presentation mid-flow and tell my audience that 'what he's not telling you is …'? Or is this partially deranged?

Later in the same presentation we are told to 'discuss how recommendation addresses the problem' which all sounds very democratic and laudable, but then we get a bit more of the ways of the world according to Bill Gates with 'discuss how plan will address hardships resulting from action'.

Well, Mr Gates, what if I don't plan to address the hardships resulting from the action, but intend instead to let everyone just deal with it? Am I allowed to use your software then? Maybe the answer is in the tiny print from hundreds of paragraphs of 'terms and conditions' of which somewhere in the long distant past I no doubt had to tick my acceptance, and which will no doubt bind me to obeisance for eternity.

Once you've composed your bad news, or good news, or your plan to invade Poland or whatever it is, PowerPoint gives you the chance to enhance your presentation with various design possibilities. Beware. This is another area which is rather like your CV – you can easily find yourself tempted into making a judgement which will tell us far more about you than the content of your visual presentation or your inarticulate garglings alongside.

These little enhancements are called things like 'Cascade' or 'Orbit', 'Stream' or 'Satellite dish', 'Mountain top' or 'Fireworks' and I could go on and on. They're all designed to convey something about you – whether you are a bit hip, in which case you are going to go for something dreamy and utterly pathetic like 'Maple', or 'Balloons'. Or maybe you are some high-powered go-getter in a hurry to embrace the future, in which case you're probably going for 'Network' or 'Echo'. You can be refined, in which case you might go for 'Refined' or you can be someone who wants to be taken seriously, in which case you very definitely won't go for any of them at all.

Oh yes, all these designs are designed to tell us something about you, and they do tell us something about you. In 99% of cases they tell us that you are a little winnet with nothing better to do with your time than to ponce around decorating your slide show.

We could go through the various different options for cutting or dissolving or animating between slides, but I think you're getting the idea. These are pathetic toys for people who enjoy meetings and think they're impressing the rest of us with their

mastery of this substitute for thought and discussion. I don't know what they do for you, but you can probably guess what they do for genuine Grumpies.

Action points

Anyway, at the end of every meeting, the Chairman will usually allocate a whole load of 'action points', which are to be noted down to be revisited at the next meeting. The trouble is that there is no time in between meetings to actually take action on the action points. So that a week passes, the meeting reconvenes, and starts with the action points from last week. Have you carried out the action points that had been assigned to you? No, of course not, there hasn't been a moment when you were not in meetings, accumulating more and more action points which had no chance of being acted upon. Has anyone else managed to put into effect the action points that had been assigned to them? Not at all, mostly for the same reason. So the same action points would be carried forward to the next meeting, with a few new ones added on at the end as a result of today's meeting.

Any other business

So what is the last word about meetings? Why have they proliferated to such an extent, and what would happen if we didn't have any meetings at all?

They have proliferated in many cases because they have become a substitute for actually doing anything. When you go from meeting to meeting to meeting, you don't ever get the chance to do anything, and so you get out of the habit of doing anything. Meetings and talking about stuff gradually seems to become so much easier than getting out there and doing it. If you talk about it, rather than actually do it, then there is a far lower possibility of failure. The only downside is that you end up employing a lot of very expensive people to sit around and talk about it, and very little actually gets done.

From time to time, some people have invented new tricks to cut down on all the waste of time and money that the proliferation of meetings inevitably causes. I once heard of an idea in which companies would have meeting rooms but with no chairs. The duration of meetings was naturally self-limiting because people got tired of standing around before they would otherwise have become tired of chatting. That strikes me as a very good idea, but it was one that didn't catch on.

And so it goes on. All you are doing is making the world go round. Oiling the wheels. Making sure people are feeling involved, kept informed, organising consensus – but you don't actually do anything. Sometimes, at the end of a typical week like this, my wife would ask me what I'd done in the last few days. Quite often I'd sit and reflect on what, if anything, had actually been achieved, and the honest answer was 'absolutely bloody nothing'. Sometimes the 'bloody' would become 'fucking', as in 'absolutely fucking nothing', but whether it was 'bloody nothing' or 'fucking nothing' was usually a function of how knackered and frustrated I felt when she asked me.

When I eventually started my own small company, I made up my mind that we would try to avoid as much of all this bollocks as possible. We wouldn't hire any idiots, wouldn't allow any politics, and we wouldn't have any meetings unless they had an actual purpose. Do you know what? We have hardly any meetings at all. We send around a weekly note telling people some key points about what's going on in the company, and we grab people during the day if we need to update on some particular project. We don't seem to have ground to a halt. They don't seem to need to be told what to do through a lot of 'action points'. Everyone just uses their brains and does what seems to be necessary. And as a result we all get a lot more done. In fact, so far as I can see, most people seem to spend most of their time in productive work.

What do you think? Any chance that this might catch on? No, I didn't think so.

Awaydays

For some employers, it doesn't seem to be enough that they own you for just the forty, fifty or sixty hours a week that you are being paid to work for them. Nor is it enough for them that they own you, mind and body. They also have to own your soul.

Notwithstanding the fact that the vast majority of your available time and energy is already dedicated to the company and all its works, it must plainly remain the case that you are spending a good proportion of whatever personal resources you may have left over with your family. Or indeed you may be spending time thinking about other matters in your life. Still worse, you may have a pursuit or hobby which distracts you from your work almost entirely.

All these are things which could easily call into question your priorities.

This allergy to the notion that you may have something of a life outside of what you do for them, applies to companies across the board, but seems to apply in particular to big corporations with more money than sense. These are the companies most likely to want you to become 'a company man' or, I suppose, 'a company woman'. I only hesitate before saying 'a company woman' because it seems to me that by and large women have more sense.

I'm talking about their penchant for 'awaydays' or, far worse, 'away-weekends'.

The purpose of these grisly events is to try to achieve something which exerts a cold grip of terror on any Grumpy worthy of the name – it's called 'bonding'. Or at least that's what it's called by the management gurus who charge a fortune to tell companies the totally bloody obvious. What we call it is unprintable even in a publication of this latitude.

Translated, I think 'bonding' means that, if you engage with your colleagues in a whole range of different ways outside of the office, this will encourage an *esprit de corp* among the staff which will, in turn, benefit the company. Presumably the notion is that you will 'go the extra mile' for a colleague if you've been up to your neck in mud and slime with him. Quite why anybody should think this is so is another question.

Typically these events are explained by the management to the poor sods who've been told that they have got to give up the last weekend in June as 'team-building'.

Now I don't know about you, but I've never been much of a one for teams. Being of a Grumpy disposition tends to mean that you don't suffer fools gladly, and if you find yourself on the same team as a bloody fool, all this does is to hold you up. I hate being held up by a bloody fool. So my instant reaction to anyone who has ever suggested spending the weekend with people from work for 'team-building' has been very similar to the feeling I get when the gastroenterologist sticks a rubber-gloved finger up my bum. It brings water to my eyes and the risk of instant evacuation of the bowels.

So not good then.

The second thing they usually say is that 'it's a chance to get to know what everyone does'. Let's leave aside the fact that, in the unlikely event that you wanted to know what everyone else does, you could very easily find out in the office. What that means is that all those people in those offices you hurry past with things like 'Business Services' on the door, and have carefully ignored for all these years, are at last going to grab the chance that has been eluding them for so long to get your more or less undivided attention.

More often than not these are the people who 'don't feel appreciated' in the company. The reason that they 'don't feel appreciated' is that they are not appreciated. Which in turn is because we don't know anything about them. Which is how we like it.

'None of you really knows what we do, but you'd certainly miss us if we were not there.' Do you know what I mean? We're talking here about the people who make sure that there are enough A4 manilla envelopes in the store cupboard or that there is a suitable variety of biscuits for important meetings. Yes yes, I know these people are important, and I know that they have a valuable job to do, but do we really have to spend hours hearing about it? And in what would otherwise be our free time?

Apparently we do.

The first big challenge facing anyone charged with organising one of these events is the venue. In my experience, one thing that managements of any big company are good at – no matter how bad they are at running the company – is looking after themselves. Despite the fact that the share price is down, revenue is plummeting, scores of the workforce are being made redundant or are having their salaries revised downwards, no compromise is to be made in the location of the awaydays. No expense is to be spared, it seems, when it comes to taking good care of the management.

The most important feature of a venue for an awayday, so far as the organisers are concerned, is that it should be remote. Certainly far enough away so that people cannot get in their car at the end of the day and spend the night at their homes.

Preferably so far from the nearest town or village that it's imprac- tical for splinter groups to head off to the nearest pub. No, usu- ally these places have to be some fortress of some kind or another. A mink-lined coffin from which there can be no escape.

So they are usually somewhere deep in the countryside, and often a part of the countryside you've never been to. Which is not a coincidence because often the reason these places tout them- selves as venues for weekend business conferences is that no-one wants to go there for any other occasion.

The other essential is that they have to have large grounds. Big areas to play games in, or in which to make an idiot of yourself. Or if I or any other Grumpy has anything to do with it, loads of places to find a quiet tree under which to sit and read a book while all this bollocks is going on.

If things are going really badly for the business, these places might even be abroad. The most fabulous weekend I ever had of this kind took place in a hotel just outside Rome – sufficiently far away in the hills to ensure that you couldn't nip out in the break to throw three coins in a fountain, but it was fabulous. Actually I think the management at Granada took a particular sadistic pleasure in the fact that the town was the ancestral home of the Forte family, whom they had just defeated in a titanic battle to take over their hotels. Holding their conference on Rocco's doorstep must have seemed too delicious to resist. Anyway, we were all treated so well on that occasion that even I don't have the stomach to take the piss. I'm just giving it as a tantalising example.

The agendas for these jaunts are usually worked out as con- sisting of a whole lot of presentations and discussions and 'break- out sessions' during the morning, a whole lot of puerile games in the afternoon, and a whole lot of awkward 'socialising' in the evenings.

Typically you'll come down to breakfast on the first morning and the first thing you notice is what people have decided to wear. How do you pitch it? Possibly something casual but not too casual? Jeans, yes, but not blue jeans. Maybe black 501s like Tony Blair wears on his days off? Nothing ripped. A nice sweat-shirt perhaps? Maybe something with the company logo on it? The office creeps have given far too much thought to what the boss is going to be wearing and the most craven of them have asked his secretary what the 'dress code' is.

There is always a lot of far-too-extended milling around at these things; coffee and orange juice and croissants, which always give you sticky fingers and there are no paper napkins so you end up wiping your hands on your agenda, just before the MD tells you he's mislaid his and can he have a look at yours.

At last everyone files into a big room, and there are rows and rows of chairs and a presentation area at the front, with a screen and one of those easels with a huge pad of white paper and lots of coloured magic markers. Oh joy. And all you are thinking is that it's bad enough that often you have to sit there and listen to all this garbage in the firm's time, but the idea that you should have to do so in time you should be spending loafing at home is as welcome to a Grumpy as a bluebottle in the ear-drum.

These occasions are the opportunity for the office dorks – especially the ones whose lives are so impoverished that they have become experts in PowerPoint – to show off by expressing their particular load of old bollocks with the help of graphs, pie-charts, animated spreadsheets or performing circus animals. Well, not performing circus animals because that would be both too entertaining and too politically incorrect, but animated graphs anyway.

These were our sales targets this year and this was our per-formance. This was our customer satisfaction quotient this year and this is what it will be next. This is what our competitors are up to, in the UK, and now in Europe, and now on the Far East and now worldwide. These are the opportunities for global domination. Here's a little film in which we've asked people in the street to give a spontaneous reaction to our product. Meanwhile, here's a little opportunity for the Grumpies among us to experience an attack of nausea and vomiting.

All this stuff goes on for what seems like hours and hours, as one office nerd after another takes to the podium and introduces what seems like his or her life-story.

During the breaks the office arse-lickers are always there to take the opportunity to collar the boss of bosses and show off how intimately they have studied the recent performance of the company's share price, and how well they understand that the recent falls have been 'with the market' so obviously they couldn't be the fault of the management. And all you can do, if you are of our disposition, is to look longingly at the programme to find out the time of the next coffee break so that you can go and sit outside for five minutes and breathe some air that hasn't been polluted by the rank smell of bullshit.

Just when you think they might be about to let you have some free time to yourself so that you can go for a solitary walk, read a book, or have a snooze, some bright-faced prune from HR announces that you're going to spend the afternoon playing silly games.

We've already said that all of these places have to have suitable outdoor space so that activities which promote 'bonding' can take place. Typically this might involve being taken to a lake or river somewhere in the grounds of the hotel, being shown a pile of wood and some rope, and being told that two teams are each going to have to build a raft and get across the water. Oh goody.

You instantly hope that the chubby kid who bored you for the last two hours with his detailed account of the workings of the health and safety department might drown. However, even this temporary diversion is dashed when it is revealed that everyone is going to have to wear a life-jacket, even though the water is only eighteen inches deep. The health and safety bloke is here, after all, and now we're all lucky enough to know what he actually does.

Over the years, when I was obliged to be involved with all this sort of shit, I developed rather a good line in seeming to receive a call on my mobile phone at the crucial moment and quickly going in to 'listening intently' mode. I would press the phone to my ear and instantly adopt a demeanour which indicates 'this is serious', and occasionally say things like 'go on', or 'just run that past me again', brow furrowed, starting to pace up and down. If colleagues showed concern I would wave my hand as if to say 'don't worry, I'm on it', but then after a little while I'd start shrugging my shoulders in a kind of 'nothing I'd rather do than be joining you to work out how to lash those two planks of wood together but I need to solve this problem' sort of way.

I would make sure that all this went on just long enough for everyone else to start getting a bit impatient, at which point I would ask my imaginary caller to hold the line just a second, put my hand over the receiver and tell them all, 'So sorry, a bit of a crisis on a shoot. You go on without me. I'll sort this out and catch you up', and then I would bolt back to the hotel for a little lie down.

Three hours later you can hear them all returning to the hotel, all covered in mud, gaiety, and sweat. Full of hilarious anecdotes about how Dotty from Accounts fell in and came up looking like the monster from Loch Ness, which, as far as I am concerned, was how she looked before she went in.

Later that evening there will usually be an informal dinner so that the most senior managers can get to know the most junior managers. One of these occasions, which I have worked hard to erase from my memory, involved having someone stick a label on your back with the name of a famous person on it. The idea, as I understand it, is that you have to guess the name on your back by asking everyone else questions, to which they could only answer yes or no. Have you done this? Good Lord.

Of course, while appearing to be a device encouraging people to break the ice and pull down the walls created by status, the actual effect of this scheme is to divide and humiliate. Certainly it used to bring hours of unconfined amusement to younger colleagues to learn that I didn't know anyone who was famous for being in *Holby City* or Duran Duran. A cause for notoriety which I have always freely embraced and in which I have forever rejoiced.

Equally, it's possible for old sods like me to raise a slight smile when it transpires that no-one under the age of forty knows who Ringo Starr is – even though in my view this simply indicates an absence of any even slight vestige of parental responsibility.

However, when it turns out that the company lawyer doesn't know who Ernest Hemingway was, and the HR person hasn't heard of Lenin (I kid you not), then it obliges you to start to re-appraise your colleagues in a whole new way. You are working with a load of bloody eejits.

So at last you get to have dinner, and if you are very lucky you might sit next to one of the few people who doesn't want to talk about how kind and generous the company is to lay on this great treat for everyone. Just as you are congratulating yourself at being with one of the few groups which doesn't seem to have been brainwashed in the cause of company loyalty, the half-wit from HR announces that all of the most senior bosses have to move around by two places to their right between each course. This is so that everyone gets a chance to do their share of creeping and saying how marvellous it all is. And if you are one of the bosses, it's one of your chances to hear what's wrong with you and the company from someone who is getting unwisely drunk and is going to be mortified in the morning, but not as mortified as you are now for having to put up with it tonight.

Eventually, everyone who wants to talk about football or speculate on whether Mandy is going to let Nick into her pants later, goes to the bar so that the rest of us can go to bed. Once in your room you breathe a sigh of relief, and maybe flick around the TV channels looking for something to take your mind off the ordeal that has been your day. The pornography channels suddenly seem inviting, but you know that they are going to appear on your room-bill as 'premium movies' and that everyone is going to know that you are a sad little tinker and start looking for warts all over your dirty little hands. So you watch the end of a crap movie and eventually doze off feeling a long long way from home, and wishing, just wishing, that you were in your own bed.

And it's another bright new dawn tomorrow.

Stress

I once ran a business which lost a million pounds a day.

Have I got your attention? I thought so, and you probably think it's another weak attempt at humour and that there is a little grumpy twist coming in the tail, but the weird thing is that – it's true. Well actually it's not quite true. In fact we would lose a million pounds for six days out of seven. I always used to say that, like God, we rested on the seventh day. We tried not to lose a million pounds on a Sunday.

You might remember something called ONdigital, latterly ITV Digital, which was the first attempt to deliver multi-channel television through your TV aerial rather than via satellite and cable. It was a joint venture business between two former ITV companies, Carlton and Granada.

Through circumstances which are far too convoluted and boring to go into here, one day I found myself as Chief Executive of this outfit. Suffice it to say that it was a job I was co-opted into rather than one I applied for. Anyway, we had large and futuristic-looking headquarters in Battersea and call centres in Plymouth and Wales. All in all we employed getting on for two thousand people and, at its height, we had well over a million customers.

Of course, losing a million pounds a day is not the way you

think of it when you are running a company like this, and even if it does occur to you in those terms, they're certainly not the words you would use if describing it to shareholders. No, in those circumstances we don't call it *losing* a million pounds a day, we call it *investing* a million pounds a day. £300 million a year, actually, because we tried not to lose, or invest, a million pounds a day on Sundays.

'Investing' is one of those words which has been given a new meaning by politicians. It sounds so much better as a use of taxpayers' money than 'spending'. 'Spending' is very bad because it feels like something that costs us all money and it has overtones of fecklessness and irresponsibility. Meanwhile 'investing' money sounds prudent and long-term, making a sacrifice today for the general good of the future.

Therefore politicians don't *spend* money on the health service, they *invest* it in the health service. Which must, of course, be bollocks because investing in something means the expectation of a return, and if you spend a couple of thousand pounds on an operation to keep a Grumpy Old Man or Woman going for a few more years after our use-by date, all you are doing is increasing the amount we are going to cost the taxpayer as we get older and more of a burden on the state, our families, and everyone around us. However, in these materialistic times when everyone is worried about the pension crisis and the cost of our increased life expectancy, maybe it's not in our interests to point this out. It's a short and ugly route to involuntary euthanasia.

Back to the point. The idea behind ONdigital was to persuade everyone who didn't already have Sky or cable to equip themselves instead with a little box that they could place under the telly. It would be connected between their aerial and the TV set, and would provide them with different packages of new TV channels. It was all jolly complicated but, in a nutshell, the system was designed to use the available airwaves more effectively, so that instead of being able to get four or five channels down your aerial and on to your screen you might be able to get up to about thirty.

All of which would probably have been fine except that, as we boasted loudly and at great length, this was a 'world-first'. While this delightful new system had worked in the laboratory and in field trials etc, no-one anywhere in the world had actually done it on an industrial scale.

Maybe one day I'll write a whole book about the ONdigital experience, except that aspects of it would be so far-fetched that no-one would think it could be anything other than fiction. However, the relevant point so far as our book on Grumpy Old

Workers is concerned is that it was a total shambles. For the simple reason that it turned out, in a nutshell, that the technology we were trying to use didn't really work. Or probably more precisely, it didn't work a lot of the time for a lot of the people, so that people who subscribed to the service frequently found that they couldn't receive the channels they were paying for. If they did receive the service, the picture would frequently freeze or fail – usually just as the centre-forward was about to take the penalty. This in turn made us very popular, especially in pubs and clubs up and down the country, most of which had pirated the service in the first place.

Not ideal then.

So in summary, the company spent the best part of a million pounds a day, an 'investment' of £300 million a year, trying to sell this service to new customers, and to put right the technical and reception problems many of them were having. This meant running marketing, sales, a whole broadcasting system, engineering, call centres, installations, etc etc etc. All in all a very big biscuit.

To be fair to us, our marketing was pretty good. Do you remember Johnny Vegas and 'Monkey'? Yes? Well that was us. Unfortunately I can't claim credit for the idea, but I do remember insisting on a few changes to the design of 'monkey' so that he looked more like a monkey and less like a pair of old socks, and a few changes to Johnny Vegas so that he looked less like an overweight vagrant and more like one of our possible paying customers. We got everyone talking about us, won an award for best advertisement of the year, and eventually the bloody monkeys were worth more as a collector's item on eBay than the digital set-top box. Last I saw of him, he was being given away with a packet of tea.

So like I say, this isn't really the time or the place to go into the whole saga, but the reason I'm including it here is to distil a lesson for Grumpy readers of this book, because losing a million pounds a day can easily be a cause of stress. Grumpies like stress about as much as we like everything else, so how do we cope with it?

And as a sub-set of the question about coping with stress, the other thing about a business like this is that, if you are not very careful, it can tend to keep you awake at night. If you are already a Grumpy Old Man or Woman and have a natural tendency to insomnia, this can be a very unfortunate thing, because it can turn what was hitherto very little sleep into absolutely no sleep at all.

I have slept badly ever since I entered my Grumpy years – in my case I was aged about twenty-five, but admittedly my Grumpiness was precocious. Perhaps surprisingly, however, running a business losing a million pounds a day did not make it especially worse. Though I was aware that it was all a big responsibility, to the customers, the shareholders and, most of all in my view, the employees, at the end of the day it was important to keep a perspective on it.

Let's call it the Grumpy perspective.

ONdigital ended up dying a long, slow, and very painful public death, and when friends, relatives, or others used to ask me how I was coping with all the sleepless nights and all the stress, I always used to say the same thing.

'No-one dies.'

Genuinely, all Grumpiness aside, I do heartily recommend this as a way of coping with the stress caused by working in business. What does it mean?

It means that if you are a train-driver and you mess up, or if you are an airplane engineer and you mess up, or if you are a nurse and you mess up, or if you are a food-processor and you mess up, then the consequences can be horrendous. These people and many others like them have all the responsibility that goes with the fact that life and death can depend on what they do, but none of them has the salary or perks of a Chief Executive of a television company. If I had to go to bed knowing that if I messed up today someone could well lose their life, or a limb, or whatever, that's what I would call stress.

Sure, losing a million pounds a day keeps you alert. It doesn't allow you a lot of relaxation. You have to get up early, work your butt off, do a lot of very hard thinking, make a lot of very difficult decisions, negotiate hard, run around, read about yourself in the financial pages, placate shareholders, and you end up every day feeling as though you have been the victim of a very serious car crash. And it's not just you. All of your colleagues are doing the same. People have mortgages to pay and investors have invested their money in good faith, so you take it seriously. But in the end no-one dies of having a poor TV reception. Unless it's from boredom at waiting for someone to come around and fix it.

In a nutshell, it's all about perspective. That's one of the benefits of Grumpiness. It can give you some perspective on the causes of stress, and therefore, perhaps surprising, many of us true Grumpies don't really stress all that much. We get Grumpy – who wouldn't? Especially when the Government could solve your problem by sorting out the digital spectrum, and even more especially when, as in this case, they waited for ITV Digital to go bust before doing exactly that so the BBC could launch Freeview. But it doesn't do to fret. Or to get stressed.

This invaluable Grumpy lesson extends a bit further into life in general. There is an enormous amount of bollocks to be concerned about somewhere near us, but by and large it's nowhere near the real and genuine bollocks which is happening to someone else who is probably not all that far away. It's about a sense of proportion. Sure we're getting on a bit and we've got a bit of arthritis coming in a finger, but no-one from the neighbouring tribe is likely to come around and chop one of our limbs off. Sure your son has an entirely unsuitable girlfriend, but there is no local outbreak of ethnic cleansing. Sure your teeth are rotting in your head and you can't find an NHS dentist, but the water supply is clean. And sure, David Cameron may well be the next Prime Minister but ... no, on second thoughts, that feels like a good reason to feel some serious stress.

But seriously though – just for a minute – it's a small small world. Taking comfort from the fact that someone somewhere else has things far worse than you isn't a particularly attractive trait, but blimey, it's difficult to get too stressed about the fact that the IT is playing up at work when 5,000 kids are dying every day of malaria.

Get Grumpy about it, by all means, but not stressed. No, not stressed.

Assorted Grumps

'Working from home'

Do you recall all those newspaper articles about how the communications revolution was going to mean that we were all able to work from home just as effectively as we could work from the office? Do you remember? All those mesmerising pieces about how our homes were going to be totally wired, and a lot of newspaper ads showing how you could convert the loft or neatly tuck your 'work-station' into a little cubby hole under the stairs? And very elegant they were too, didn't you think, with all that laminate?

There would be so many of us working from home that employers were going to be able to reduce the number of desks in the office. Travel would be so much easier because we could all be totally in touch from our houses, and therefore few of us would be obliged to do the daily commute.

How's that going, do you think?

Well to find the answer you just have to try to get from your home to work any time between seven and nine in the morning. Sitting in three lanes of traffic, nose to tail, millions of worker ants sweeping in and out of town like a marauding army every day, it doesn't feel as though an inordinate number of people are working from home. It feels like there are about four times as many people as the world can accommodate all trying to use the roads at the same time. All rushing backwards and forwards in and out of the ant-hill. Swarms of them.

That's not to say that most of us are not fully wired in our homes in the way that was foreseen. That little spare space which might once have been dedicated to a hobby or a wine-store is now fully kitted out with screen and keyboard and a natty designer desk-lamp and in- and out-trays and the rollerdeck and the printer and other associated kit. In extreme cases, the shed or the out-house or even the former barn has become a branch office at the free-of-charge disposal of our employers.

If it wasn't enough that we had to have our telly working, and our washing machine working, and our telephone working, nowadays we've got to have our bloody broadband working, and what kind of an ordeal is that? Think about it. How much time have you actually spent in the last five years fiddling about try-ing to get the internet connection in your home to work properly? If you can honestly say 'very little' in response to that question, then trust me, you should be counting yourself as a very very lucky person indeed. If, like me, it has added up to hours and hours going into days of trying to do exactly what it is they seem to have asked you to do, single-clicking here and double-clicking there, but still not connecting, and then hanging on the tele-phone for about half your lifetime, then you'll empathise. And local area networks? Don't even get me started.

It just means that we are not working from home *instead* of working at the office, we are working from home *as well as* working from the office.

Whereas at one time you would have to stay at work until that vital fax came in from New York, deal with it, and then go home, put your feet up, have a glass of wine and fall asleep in front of the telly; now you can indeed leave the office at the same time as everyone else. It's just that as soon as you get home, you have to head for the little alcove or hole in the wall or whatever it is, and turn on the computer to see what messages you might have missed during your two-hour commute.

Say a quick hello on your way through the door, a peck on the cheek, and straight to the home-office, and 'switch on, boot up, and log-in' – the 21st-century equivalent to Dr Timothy Leary's advice from forty years earlier. Take a look in the in-box and there it is. The awaited message from New York. Inevitably there are five other messages which have popped into your in-box as well, and you just need to deal with them before you can sit down and have your fish-fingers. Yes yes, your partner is calling from the kitchen that your meal is ready; 'just be a minute hun', but this urgent message from the US has come with a bloody huge attachment and the hour-glass is working away as hard as it can but the thing is showing no sign of opening any time this side of *Newsnight*.

'Food is on the table!'

'Yes yes, just a minute. I'll be there in a minute,' and still the thing is downloading at the speed of a salted slug and you are certain that any moment you're going to die of frustration. Oh and by the way, this is the part of the day when you were sup-posed to start to relax.

The next thing is that one of the kids is sent in to get you and whispers something like 'Mum's getting cross', and so you tear yourself away from the screen and try to concentrate on eating your food and on pretending to be interested in everyone's day. But you can't really focus on the food and everyone's day because you know that you still have to deal with this ball-aching message from New York, and that it has probably downloaded by now, and that on the other side of the Atlantic they're waiting for you to reply – and probably wondering why there is the delay because, after all, it's only 7.30 p.m. in the UK, and so you should still be in the office.

You know that you aren't really giving full attention to the family, and the family knows it too.

'What was that dear?'

'Hmm? Oh sorry, wasn't listening.' Sound familiar?

By now you have undoubtedly reached another major milestone on your journey towards the inevitable duodenal ulcer, and you are ready to 'just go and finish this off', so that we can all relax for the rest of the evening. Promise.

Back in the cubby-hole, you get to work just sorting out all this last minute stuff and, before you know where you are, it's half past ten, the kids have gone out or gone to bed, and your partner is sitting on his or her own, watching the telly, eating pistachio nuts, and entirely pissed off. And who can blame them?

No, the so-called office revolution and 'working from home' has worked out to be yet another con-trick to make us all work harder. To make us work in what was at one time considered to be our own time instead of the boss's time. And of course, that's not even to mention all the additional pieces of bondage equipment which have made it impossible for us ever to be free of the dominatrix that pays our wages. Yes, I'm talking about the mobile phone, the pager, and the dreaded bloody BlackBerry.

It was bad enough when it was only the mobile phones which could call you to prayer at any time of the day or night. Now our worship of work can be called upon by a vast range of ever lighter and more functionary laptops and personal organisers and MP3 downloads and all sorts of devices of the BlackBerry variety. And now half the world is spending half their time squinting into a screen that's far too small to be able to read, and orchestrating every detail of their lives with a blur of twiddling thumbs.

You can never get away from it; never turn it off. It follows you everywhere. The bloody BlackBerry is the first thing to be switched on with the coffee percolator in the morning, and the last thing to be switched off with the bedside light at night. If then. An electronic ball and chain, and we're all doomed to be prisoners.

Meanwhile, for the lucky few, the idea of 'working from home' actually has some meaning. The expression has become a wonderful euphemism which roughly translates into 'doing a lot of pissing about and being unable to walk past the fridge without opening it and making yourself a snack'. When I first left ITV and was in the process of setting up Liberty Bell, I did quite a bit of working from home, and I put on about a stone in weight.

I'm not sure why it is, but it seems to me that it's just not possible to sit there in your own house, and to work continually without frequently getting up, going for a wander around, flicking around the controls on the telly, looking up Amazon to see when the next series of the *Sopranos* is coming out on DVD, making a cup of tea and just fixing a little cheese and pickle sandwich while we're at it. Maybe there are some people who are far more self-disciplined than I am who can manage it, but if so, I've never met them.

I love it when I call up a broadcaster or any other business and someone's assistant says they are 'working from home today'. It's like the idea that they are just having a bloody day off would be so unthinkable, that the excuse has to be there right up-front so no-one would think they were guilty of taking some time for themselves. No-one ever has a day off. They're all 'working from home'. Which actually gives real 'working from home' a bad name (like I care).

'Sickies'

'Sickies' on the other hand do have the effect of pissing off Grumpies. It's a horrible expression, and one which seems to have entered common parlance at an unwelcome and inordinate speed. So much so that it even seems to be OK to refer to 'sickies' in the TV news when we get those all-too-regular stories about surveys showing what a load of bone-idle freeloaders we have all become.

Even worse than the expression 'sickies' is the phrase 'throw a sickie', which seems to me to be unnecessarily vivid and horribly unpleasant. I gather that it means what happens when you wake up a bit poorly and call in sick rather than make the effort to come to work.

If I'd been inclined towards that sort of thing as a younger man I never would have gone to work at all. In those days I used to drink rather more than I do today, and would wake up feeling like shit every day of my life. But what did I do? I got up and went to work, and by about mid-morning I usually started feeling reasonably human. If, instead of just feeling the after-effects of alcohol it turned out that I was actually ill, well by that time I was at work anyway, so just had to get on with it.

These days you just have to laugh when you ask where someone is and the reply is 'they've got a cold' or 'they've got a tummy upset'. When I hear that I just want to say 'If they want a day off, they can probably have one. I just prefer not to be patronised with any bollocks about 'running a temperature'.' But of course you can't do that, because that implies that you don't believe what your employees tell you, and that would never do.

Still more irritating even than any of that, if you are trying to run any sort of business, is when you switch on breakfast telly and see reports of a little local difficulty on public transport, or a flurry of snow, or a plague of frogs or whatever, and the newsreader says 'the advice is that if you don't have to go out today, stay at home'. Oh thank you. You've just given permission for thousands of people to stay off work today because 'it said so on the telly'. Maybe you would be kind enough also to explain to the bank manager that you told all my staff to stay at home, which is why I can't repay his loan?

The email of the species is deadlier than the mail

I reckon that email has been responsible for more misunderstandings, rows, and debacles of one kind or another than anything since office juniors discovered that inhaling stencil fluid could give them a high before it eventually made them go blind.

I mean, whoever invented something that could enable you to write a note telling your boss to 'go fuck yourself', and send it within the space of about two seconds, should be hacked to death with a blunt machete. If that facility had been available to me when I was thirty, I would have been fired so many times that I would have ended up totally unemployable. The same would apply to most of the Grumpy Old Men of my acquaintance.

Who doesn't want to tell the boss to go piss up a rope from time to time? But the point about the old memo system was that you had a chance to think about it, to reflect on the wisdom of it, and to repent at leisure. Instant email means that you have told the stupid old sod what you think of his latest note or idea in the twinkling of an eye – and by the way, the 'retrieve' facility very seldom works. I know. I've tried it.

The risk of telling the truth to the boss isn't the only drawback of email. The combination of instant 'reply' and predictive texting, where if you start to type in 'Peter' it'll suggest the first 'Peter' from your address list to send it to, is just asking for trouble, isn't it? We've all heard of those well-reported examples of idiots who intend to send a memo about colleague A to colleague B, but send it to colleague A instead, thereby inadvertently informing colleague A that someone is sleeping with his girlfriend.

Worse than that have been the many examples of what were supposed to have been private notes to colleague C being distributed to everyone else (colleagues D–Z) in the company, or indeed sometimes everyone in the bloody world.

And it's so tempting. So very tempting! All that power at your disposal with just a twitch of a finger. Have you ever driven along a busy A road with traffic coming towards you at high speed and reflected on how very dire are the consequences that would result of just the smallest flick of the wrist? You haven't? Maybe I shouldn't have mentioned it.

Well anyway, I reckon the same goes for email. There is something strangely compelling about the ability to affect so much damage by an otherwise almost imperceptible tick of a finger. It must be rather like the power felt by the Caesars of ancient Rome. A thumb up or a thumb down and the Christian's life could be spared or snuffed. Same here. A left click on the mouse while the cursor hovers over 'send' and careers can be ruined, marriages ended, wars started.

Scary stuff, I think you'll agree.

Competitive tiredness

When I get home from the office, my wife will usually ask me what sort of a day I've had and, being of a grumpy persuasion, I almost always give her a nice grunt and say 'shattering' or something similar. What I actually mean is that I have had a series of meetings, or have sat in an editing room, or attended a conference of some sort, and that's my idea of hard work.

However, the reason I have to describe the results of this as 'shattering' is because, obviously, I'm a bloke and I need to be cosseted and fussed over when I get home in the evening. I don't mean fussed over in the sense of messed about with. I don't want anyone stroking my arm or patting my head, for heaven's sake. However, I do mean fussed over in the sense that secretly I'd like to think someone would put my slippers out next to the door – the way that my grandmother used to do for my grandfather.

Obviously this has to be a secret desire because this kind of thing is not approved of in our house nor, I'm told, in the world in general. It's the 21st century, apparently, and the idea of a patriarchal father coming in from work and finding the family all lined up and grateful that he is putting a roof over heads and food on the table, is long out of date. I guess I can understand that, and I guess I approve of it, but somewhere deep down the Grumpy in me has some regrets.

The other reason that I have to establish straight away that I am 'shattered' is that of course it has to be clear that I am more tired than my wife is – whatever kind of a day she has had. This is a bit easier now than it used to be because, truth to tell, these days neither of us really works our bottoms off, but it was not always thus.

When the kids were younger, and my wife would regularly have a terrible day running around after them, tidying up, cooking, shopping, cleaning, washing, ironing, doing their homework, bathing them, putting them to bed etc, and I would have a day at my desk, this was not so easy. Indeed, sometimes the imbalance would be so pronounced that, when I got in from work at 7 p.m. or even later, she might not even ask me how my day had been. I could tell from a glance that hers had been a lot harder than mine.

Even still, there is something about men in general, and Grumpy Old Men in particular, that needs to go in for 'competitive tiredness'. You know what it's like.

'I'm tired.'

'You're tired? I'm tired.'

'Yes but I'm so tired I could sleep standing up.'

'Really? I'm so tired I could sleep on the end of a branch on that tree.'

'Yeah? I'm so tired I could sleep on a cactus.'

'Oh? I could sleep on a cactus with a jackdaw pecking at my privates.'

'Yeah? I'm so tired I could sleep on a cactus with someone

hammering electrified pins into my eyeballs ...' and so on and so on.

The reason that both sides want to win this battle is that, in every household and every relationship, there is a certain amount of what I call 'discretionary running around' when both partners are at home towards the end of the day.

There are things which are undoubtedly her job. Stuff like making the dinner, clearing away the plates, stacking the dish-washer, emptying the spin-drier, feeding the cat and clearing the shit out of its litter tray. Then there are all the things that are undoubtedly my job, like pouring a glass of wine or making sure the doors are locked or switching off the television standby light. (The best thing about global warming is that whereas to do this used to be an indication of how mean I was, nowadays I can pre-tend that I do it because of my concern for the future of the planet.)

But between the jobs that are undoubtedly mine and the jobs that are undoubtedly hers, there are a few tiny tasks which may fall to whichever of us has lost the battle of competitive tiredness, and neither of us wants to do them. Which one of us, for exam-ple, is responsible for closing the cat-flap? Or for bringing up fresh drinking water for the bedside tables? Which one is going to set the burglar alarm? All these may seem trivial when it's just written on the page here, but these are some of the politics of a marriage which make the world go round.

Competitive tiredness, my dear fellow Grumpies: be sure to win the battle.

Office parties

The very idea of an office party is oxymoronic, and it seems to me that anyone who can honestly say they enjoy them must be one of Oxy's less interesting siblings.

Like a family Christmas, office parties throw you together

with a whole load of people who may be the last people on earth with whom you would choose to socialise, and then force you to try to have a good time. I'm not sure if anyone can truly have a good time in such circumstances, but if there is such a person he or she is assuredly not of the Grumpy persuasion.

Let's face it, we already spend more of our waking hours with these people than is good for us. More than we do with our wives, our kids, or our mates. We have to sit cheek by ever-slackening jowl with them during the day, we have to rub shoulders with them in the lift, and most likely we have to queue with them in the staff canteen or the local sandwich shop. We might find ourselves commuting with one of them, taking a coffee break with another of them, and even occasionally going for a swift drink after work with others of them.

These are people with whom fate just happens to have thrown us together.

In many other ways too, we are obliged to treat people at work as though they were as close as our loved ones. For example, pressure of the job when the kids were younger meant that I never got time to go to any of the parties which my wife held for their birthdays. But when someone I hardly know in the office has a birthday I'm compelled to look on with an apparent smile as he or she very cleverly blows out candles on an iced cake hastily purchased from Marks and Spencer, and to try to think of something witty to cram in amid the obscenities scrawled all over a giant greetings card.

When one of them is getting married we have to make a contribution to some preposterous gift. When another of them has a baby, we have to stand around with a glass of warm wine and ooh and aah over terrible photos of a pink squawking blur.

So having forcibly become far more intimate with work colleagues than one could ever wish to, and certainly to spend far more time with them than any sensible person would wish, why oh why would we then want to go to a party with them? The answer is of course obvious, and goes to the heart of the horror that is the office party for a Grumpy. Places of work, as most of us who have spent a lot of time in them are aware, are barely concealed cauldrons of lust.

The twenty- and thirty-year-old blokes with not enough actual work to do have few diversions other than to spend the whole year wondering what colour panties Becky wears, and to speculate on whether that gravity-defying uplift is caused by a particularly well-engineered bra or whether it could conceivably be her natural shape. The women, I am reliably informed, spend unbelievable amounts of time wondering if that bulge is just the way that Martin's trousers are cut, or whether he could actually be that size.

The office party is the one chance in twelve months to find out.

Over the years, I've worked in a number of places where the office party at Christmas is notorious for its excess, and you have to say that the sense of anticipation in these places is tangible. Some time in the afternoon, a group of volunteers will start clearing away desks and filing cabinets, or the tables and chairs in the staff canteen. Maybe a 'disco' will arrive and it turns out that the nerd from the post-room with the dodgy haircut is secretly a part-time or would-be 'DJ', and we're going to start viewing him in a whole different way from tomorrow. From over in another corner there will be occasional loud bangs and fits of giggles as idiots over-blow balloons, and somewhere else people are standing on wobbly stepladders and draping streamers over fluorescent bulbs, thereby creating what will later become a fire hazard.

All the girls have brought a little overnight bag comprising a very small compartment containing what they're going to be wearing later and a very large compartment for their make-up and condoms. Around about 4 p.m. the female secretaries start vacating their desks and head off to the ladies room to begin their preparations, and the young blokes head off to the pub to begin theirs. The scene is set for a bacchanalian orgy of prurience and puke.

Nice.

The Grumpies among us try to keep ourselves to ourselves while all this is going on, and determine to arrive late and/or to leave early. However, it seems that we cannot be allowed to do so secretly. Doreen from Accounts will inevitably make it her business to enquire whether we are going to be our usual miserable selves this evening, and will ensure that our grunted replies are broadcast far and wide. 'Old Miggins is being his usual spoilsport self – has brought his car and says he's "got an early start in the morning".' Thank you Doreen. Kind of you to let everyone know my escape plans.

It's all going to go exactly how you think it's going to go. Over the following six hours, a load of middle-aged blokes who should know better are going to be getting drunk and throwing their wobbly bodies around the dance floor in a sad and anarchic parody of Mick Jagger. Women who usually do know better are spilling out of dresses which were unwise even as they put them on when sober, and are getting less and less wise as barely constrained bulges make their bids for freedom. Deafening music, floors sticky with spilled beer, and voices getting ever louder. The veritable definition of hell for a Grumpy.

There will be nudging and pointing as the strobe light tracks the staccato progress of Michael's hands en route to an area of Babs's anatomy where no hand would ordinarily be allowed. Dark alcoves and cleaners' rooms and stationery cupboards will be put to uses far from those in the minds of the architects.

For some reason, the idea of having someone I don't like much yelling indecipherable bollocks while spitting beery saliva into my face or into my ear has always held limited appeal for me. This, and the fact that I have long been of the Grumpy persuasion, means that I've always chosen a moment to make my exit well before any of this has become really embarrassing.

An early exit, however, does not always protect one from the excruciating consequences arising from these occasions. Once, when I was CEO of a certain well-known TV company, it was drawn to my attention that the security guys had a video featuring a certain senior executive and his current assistant engaging in an activity in the underground car park which was well outside her job description and, now I come to think about it, was well outside of his as well. The Head of Security, it turned out, was a 'job's-worth' who felt that his staff's morals may have been corrupted by this trauma and was keen to 'take it further' – whatever that meant. Can you imagine how much fun it is trying to deal with that sort of shite?

No, the thought of an office party fills Grumpies with cold, paralysing horror. We don't want to go there. We just don't.

'You don't know when you are well off'

What's the worst job you've ever had?

I only ask because sometimes when Grumpy Old Men and Grumpy Old Women are being more than usually grumpy, we have to put up with other people reminding us that 'you don't know when you are well off'. The idea is, apparently, to remind us that we shouldn't be complaining because there are a lot of people in the world worse off than we are.

How does that work for you?

I've always thought it a rather unattractive human trait that we feel better knowing that someone else is worse off than we are. Why should that make us feel better? It should make us feel worse. We're in this situation and feeling bloody depressed about it – how much better should it make you feel to know that someone else is in a worse situation and feeling even more depressed?

More likely of course this little stricture is accompanied by '… and you don't hear him complaining'. That's usually because if the poor bugger is in Indonesia or Bangladesh, we wouldn't hear him if he was complaining. And if he did complain, and we did hear him, the likelihood is that his boss would make his situation even worse.

But I think it was Arlo Guthrie who originally asked us to think about the last guy. The last guy. All of us take comfort in the idea that someone has it worse than we do, but think about the last guy. Nobody has got it worse than him. Which brings us to the question of what is the worst job you ever had.

It's a perennially amusing concept which I think first appeared on my radar with the legendary performances of Peter Cook and Dudley Moore in *Derek and Clive (Live)*. Hilarious if also utterly vile improvised stuff between the two of them in which each vied for the accolade of having had a worse job than the other.

I can't remember the whole thing, but I think that one of Dud's best contenders involved him recalling his work picking the bogies off Winston Churchill's bedspread. What with all those big cigars etc, it seems that Winston Churchill used to produce these most enormous bogies, and someone had to go and remove them from his bedclothes. So large were they, it was said, that you could go to sea in them, which was not always a reliable form of water-borne transport. 'Never go to sea on a bogie' was a piece of advice which I, for one, have always followed and consistently found useful.

The winning entry, though, was a job which I think Peter Cook said he once had in which his duties were picking the lobsters out of Jayne Mansfield's bum. She was a lovely girl, according to Peter, 'lovely bum, lovely tits, but she did have these fucking great big lobsters up her arsehole', an image which, if you haven't heard it before, will stay with you. As indeed it has stayed with me.

The theme came up again in slightly less graphic form recently when one of the 'talking points' on the BBC News website asked surfers to say what had been the worst job they had ever had. Maybe most of them were too gross to be reproduced by the BBC, but actually I thought the ones they showed were fairly mimsy:

'Working on a day cruise boat (that had a bad roll, and pitched from side to side) in choppy water. Dealing with an endless amount of sick passengers', was the contribution from Louise from Sydney which, the website helpfully informed us, is in Australia.

Alun E Williams, from 'the UK', took the trouble to write in to say that 'the worst one I had was shelf stacking in a major super-market chain. I worked on night shifts under two supervisors who came straight out of a Charles Dickens novel'. Stacking shelves eh? Pretty bloody awful.

The only one I thought was even a contender was from some-one called Jon Hanson who said:

'Quality control on cat food. Test 1: Bury face in a huge tub of it and sniff it to make sure it's fresh. Test 2: Plunge arms in it up to the elbows and grope for bony bits and take them out. Test 3: Scoop up huge dollop of it, smear it flat on surface and prod it with fingers to test how much gristle is there. Uggghh!'

OK, I concede that that's right up there. However, it feels as though there is very little these days to compare with some of the historic 'worst evers' which I see are being rehearsed by the ever-lovely Tony Robinson in a new TV series. I think the idea is that he is going to try a few of them, but there are at least a couple on the list which he isn't going to try. One was the task of a 17th-century doctor whose job included tasting other people's wee.

In those days, apparently, the whole of medicine was based on the 'four humours', meaning patients were either sanguine, phlegmatic, choleric or melancholic. When I started reading that short list I felt a frisson of excitement that maybe Grumpiness was going to have been diagnosed as a clinical condition several hundred years ago, thereby undermining my patent. In fact Grumpiness wasn't itemised separately, but I have it down as a sub-set of 'choleric'. Anyway, it seems that one of the best ways of finding out which of the four humours dominated was to do a little taste test on the person's wee. Which is nice.

However, even that seems to me to be the equivalent of dressing-room attendant at Spearmint Rhino in comparison to the other medieval honour, which was called 'The Groom of the Stool'. This person was basically Henry VIII's chief bum-wiper. He had to crouch down behind the bench or whatever it was functioned as a latrine in those days, and clean the royal arse-hole. And it seems that if you didn't do a good job first time around then you could always mop it up with what was called a diper, which was actually a diamond-shaped piece of linen with a pattern on it. Hence, presumably, the origin of the word 'diaper'.

You see? All this is educational as well as everything else. Where else would you have learned that?

The strange thing about the 'Groom of the Stool' is that you'd think it would be allocated to someone who had royally pissed off the majestic personage, but quite the contrary. So intimate did you necessarily become with the King, that only favoured courtiers were chosen to do it. Which is a useful lesson for any-one tempted to become the office creep.

Time to Leave

ere's a free tip. If you don't want to give up your job, don't resign.

It doesn't sound like much of a piece of advice, does it? Seems kind of obvious, but just think about it for a moment, and then think about the number of apparently sensible people you know who haven't followed it.

Have a think, for example, about David Blunkett. How much of a twerp did he make of himself over that stupid American woman and her son and her nanny and all that stuff? I used to have a bit of a soft spot for old David Blunkett. I think he went a bit mad when he was Education Secretary and a bit madder still when he was Home Secretary, but basically I had always thought of him as a man with his heart in the right place. More or less.

But do you remember what you felt when you heard that he had been having an affair with that dreadful American woman? Kimberly Quinn was it? Part of you is thinking that it's a bit weird that an American heiress finds a raddled old git like Blunkett attractive, and part of you is thinking 'good for you David, nice that you are getting your end away'. Or perhaps you were thinking something more refined than that.

Then of course it gets in the newspapers because he has helped out his girlfriend's nanny, or he hasn't helped out his girlfriend's nanny, or maybe he has or maybe he hasn't. Basically you don't give a damn because all sensible people understand that there's very little point in having all that power if you don't use it to help out your mates once in a while.

Then all of a sudden, old Blunkett ups and resigns. Sure, the newspapers were all over him like an embarrassing rash, but who in their right mind would care about that? I always thought you had to develop a thick skin to be a politician. Quits his job. After all that time sitting in dingy local council chambers in Sheffield, and all those horrible years as a backbench MP, he finally gets the gig he's wanted all along and he ups and resigns.

We're all feeling a bit sorry for David and that he's been a bit hard done by, when he starts coming out with all that old tosh about 'I'm resigning, but I've done nothing wrong', and so then you start to wonder. What on earth is he talking about? Did you do something wrong, or didn't you? If you did, shut up, and if you didn't, why did you resign?

In a rare wish to get some facts right I looked this up on the BBC website, and it's worth quoting a little bit from it:

> In an emotional interview with BBC Political Editor Andrew Marr, Mr Blunkett said: 'I did not in August initiate the terrible trauma of my relationship (with ex-lover Kimberly Quinn) coming to the fore.
>
> 'I did not in late November start the plethora of linking my private life with public events again.
>
> 'I am mortified that that was done and I am very sorry. I'm not even angry, I'm just terribly hurt and I want people to know that in my public life I have always tried to help people.'

See what I mean? Here's a bloke who plainly loves his job, wants to take every opportunity to remind us that he has done nothing wrong, but says he's resigning anyway. And all the way from thinking 'pity about poor old David' immediately we are thinking

'what a plonker!' Because you know that at some level he's imagining that this 'I've never done anything wrong but am going
because I'm a man of honour' line will cause a groundswell of
public opinion which is going to force him, apparently reluc-
tantly and protesting all the way, to stay on. We're all going to
feel so bad that this honourable man has indeed been so honourable that he has felt compelled to resign from a job he adores,
that we'll all rush up to him as one and say, 'no no David, we
really wouldn't hear of it. You mustn't go. You're a man of enormous integrity. We simply won't let you.'

Well of course that didn't happen. Everyone just thought 'if
you've done nothing wrong, what are you resigning for?' and did
nothing about it.

So then David Blunkett began his campaign to get back into
the Cabinet. Within minutes, it seems, of the Prime Minister
accepting his resignation, Blunkett is on the telly talking about
how 'if the Prime Minister should see fit, in his infinite wisdom,
to bring me back into a senior role within the Government, who
am I – a man of great integrity who has, after all, never done anything wrong – to deny the British people my services?' Or words
to that effect.

Actually, I've now looked up his actual words, and they're
worse than the ones I made up for him. What he actually said was
that Mr Blair had *backed me to the hilt*, adding: *'I have built my
reputation on honesty, I have sometimes been too honest.'*

'Too honest'? Oh groo.

So just when you thought it was all over and we could get on
with being irritated by Charles Clarke instead of David Blunkett,
the extraordinary and sorry saga continued because after about
fifteen minutes good old Tony gave Blunkett a job as Minister for
Work and Pensions, whatever that is. Sounds more like a job
from the Attlee Government than the Blair one, but there we are.
But bugger me, ten minutes after that he resigns again. This time

it's because he has some shares in a futuristic-sounding business called DNA Biosphere and shouldn't have, allegedly. Once again, apparently, David is resigning on a matter of honour, rather than because he has done anything wrong.

'I step down today precisely to protect the Government from diversion, from the policies that we are carrying out, from the reforms we are bringing in.'

So, David, have you done something wrong this time, or haven't you?

'Those accusations were unfounded, as was the suggestion that I had had dealings with and made representations on behalf of DNA Bioscience.'

So, is the answer 'no'? Apparently not. It seems that the problem wasn't having the shares, it was that he didn't mention it at the appropriate moment. Or something. At last he has done something wrong, perhaps.

'So I am guilty of a mistake and I am paying the price for it and I make no bones about saying that it is my fault and I stand by it.'

But David hasn't finished.

'Let me just say this: I am extremely proud of what I have been able to do over the last eight years.'

Yes yes, we're fed up with you now. Are you going or aren't you?

So you see what I meant at the beginning of the chapter? If ever there was a bloke whose life was defined by his work, it was David Blunkett. He did not want to resign on either occasion, and certainly didn't want the Prime Minister to accept his resignations, but he did so anyway. And where is he now? Nowhere. That's where he is now.

Greg Dyke is another one. You remember? Used to be Director General of the BBC? Now I know Greg Dyke a bit. Actually he's a mate in a sort of a way. Like most of us, he's made a bit of a dick of himself from time to time but I've always had a soft spot for him, and certainly most of the programme-makers liked him. But when Alastair Campbell attacked the BBC's journalism in the Gilligan row, Greg Dyke followed his instincts rather than his common sense, and told the Government to fuck off.

Telling the Government to fuck off in these circumstances is almost always a good idea if you are a broadcaster, but the best thing to do is to first make sure you are right. Greg made the mistake of telling the Government to fuck off before he checked that the BBC was right, and it turned out that the BBC wasn't right. So Greg Dyke did what appeared to be the honourable thing and resigned.

No sooner had he done so than the staff piled out onto the street in his support. They didn't want to lose their programme-loving DG just because he had stood up for BBC journalism. But then something unexpected happened. The staff carrying Greg shoulder-high were carrying him outside. After all, he had resigned, so they presumed that this was the appropriate direction. However, being carried out wasn't the plan at all. Greg had allowed himself to believe that the welter of popular support would carry him shoulder-high back into the building. This was going in altogether the wrong direction.

It turned out that Greg thought the BBC Governors would not accept his resignation but, in the event, they did. Cue collapse of otherwise excellent plan. And since then Greg has made perfectly clear that he didn't want to resign, and wished he had his job back, and it was the best job in the world, etc etc etc.

See what I mean? Another example of a bloke resigning who didn't really want to give up his job. I could go on and on. Two Mandelson resignations from the Cabinet, in much the same tone as the Blunkett cases, all couched in that 'I've done nothing wrong but I'm resigning anyway' language which makes the rest of us so bilious. Ron Davies – he's another one – didn't do anything wrong either, apparently, but well, you know, just had to go – and five minutes later he wanted his job back. What a berk.

Obviously for most of us mere Grumpies, the decision whether or not to resign is less of a public one than in the examples I've given, but the principle is the same. Never resign on a matter of principle unless you genuinely don't mind going. If your general idea is that people will be so horrified by your possible departure, or so impressed by your integrity, that they will urge you to stay, don't go there. Because the chances are that some dick-head somewhere will accept. Someone you hadn't thought about will secretly have been wanting your job and will offer to do it for half what you were earning. Or they were thinking of making you redundant anyway, and now they don't have to pay you off. Or maybe they just don't give a damn if you stay or go.

So don't resign unless you really want to and, preferably, have another job to go to. OK?

Getting fired, on the other hand, is another matter altogether.

One of the worst things about being the boss is that occasionally you have to tell people they are losing their jobs. I've probably had to do it a dozen times or so in my career, and it's undoubtedly the worst aspect of any job. However bad it is, though, I don't think bosses giving people the sack are going to get a lot of sympathy, and especially not in comparison to the people on the receiving end.

Having fired some people and had them take it well, and having fired other people and had them take it badly, my advice to anyone on the receiving end of being fired is to take it well. This is by far and away the way most guaranteed to achieve what should at this point be your first objective – to make the boss feel like shit. And, indeed, to make him wonder if maybe he has made a mistake.

In fact, over the years I've come to the view that you find out so much more about a person's character when they are losing their job than you do when they are being given their job. When they are getting their job, everyone is happy, everything is promising, everyone is very cheerful and full of 'many thanks for the opportunity – I won't let you down'.

But when a person has let you down, or worse, hasn't let you down but circumstances arise which mean they can no longer stay in the job, everything is very different.

If this happens to you, and you find yourself on the receiving end of the speech, your natural reaction can easily be to recriminate. Heaven knows it would be understandable if you did feel that way. Some bastard in a suit calls you in for what you are expecting to be news about your latest pay-rise or time off or request for holidays, and starts by looking at his shoes and saying something like, 'I'm afraid I've got something rather difficult to say to you.'

Your instinctive feeling when he has finished what is almost always going to be patronising rubbish is obviously to break something, maybe something on or about his person. Short of that, you may wish to respond in kind. You may be inclined to point out that the reason the company is in difficulties and that people like you have to go is because of the incompetence of people like him; and that if there was any justice in the world, it would be him that was going, not you or people like you. Or you might just want to tell him where he can stick his tin-pot little job that you didn't want to do anyway.

All of these are tempting, but trust me, none of them achieves your objective as effectively as the alternative I am going to recommend. It is this.

If and when you find yourself getting fired, you should do

your best to sit and listen calmly. Try not to interrupt, so that after he has gone through all the platitudes about it hurting him more than it's hurting you, and hoping that you will understand his predicament, he may feel that he has to go on speaking to fill the silence. Then he may well end up saying far more than he ever intended. About how it isn't your fault, and that maybe he has made some mistakes, and it is a pity that others have to pay for them, etc etc.

When eventually you are sure he has nothing else to say, you should continue to remain silent for a further second or two, and then simply stand up, and say something like: 'Well thank you for taking the time and trouble to tell me about this yourself. It can't have been easy for you. I think you are making a big mistake, but you are the boss and I am not, so I guess you know what you are doing. I hope so because I think you are in breach of my contract so I'll be contacting my lawyer. But meanwhile, good luck.'

Then you should turn, leave, go straight to your desk, empty it, and exit the building saying nothing to anyone.

I guarantee that you will have left him feeling like a total and utter bastard.

Any time anyone has done this or something like it to me, my immediate thought has been that I had made a mistake. This bloke obviously had far more character, far more about him, than I had given him credit for. Maybe I was wrong to have fired Smith instead of Jones. Maybe I should reinstate Jones and fire Smith instead. Of course I never have reinstated Jones, but I certainly have spoken highly of him to others, and have probably given Jones a far better reference for his next job than otherwise I might have done. Cold comfort, maybe, if you are getting fired anyway, but certainly a better way to leave than to be dragged out by the security guards kicking and screaming and trying to grip on to the leg of your desk.

No, losing a job is seldom fun, and if it happens to you it can

very easily contribute significantly to the grumpiness of the Grumpy Old Man or Woman. Knowing that you have handled it well, however, can ease the pain.

Grumpy? Of course we are. The guy who fired you isn't worthy to shine your shoes. But do we bear a grudge? Of course we do – what, do you think we're completely mad?

The Final Question

I think I said somewhere near the beginning that one of the key features of Grumpy Old Men and Women is that we tend to question all the stuff that everybody else seems to find obvious. We're not being cantankerous deliberately; it's just the way our brains work.

I gave a few examples earlier, I think, but as we're revisiting the subject, let's see if we can think of another one.

It said on the news this morning that the latest development in the absolutely extraordinary 'Big Brother' world in which we live is that the operators of closed circuit surveillance systems are going to start shouting at us. Yes that's right. They're adding speakers to all those already totally and outrageously intrusive spy-cameras which are on every street corner and shopping mall and the idea is that, if they see someone doing something they don't like, a tinny voice is going to shout 'hoy, you in the red jumper, pick up that litter' or 'you can't park that bike against those railings' or whatever.

As I write I can also almost hear half the neighbourhood saying 'Yes, and a bloody good thing too. Time to get tough on the hooligans.' I know where you're coming from (as they, rather irritatingly, say), but as a Grumpy Old Man, all I'm thinking is, 'what the hell?'

If it's not bad enough that we are spied upon for practically every minute of every day, monitored, checked, looked-into, surveyed, interfered with and probed. If it's not bad enough that we've got the real police and the community police and the neighbourhood watch and the traffic wardens and the tax inspectors and the social services and the welfare people and the TV licence people and the congestion charge people and the internet-police or whatever they're called, sticking their vile proboscis into the most minute details of our behaviour. If all that's not enough, now the thought-police are going to start ordering us about in the street by remote control. Just like we were back in the playground and the head teacher was going to glance out of the staff-room window as we kick the ball in a part of the yard that is out of bounds. 'Hey you, Dawdle, see me in my office.'

We're grown-ups, presumably responsible, have a job, pay our dues, in many cases have brought up families, and some tin-pot know-nothing ill-informed, under-educated, red-necked, shithead secreted in a little booth where he mostly preoccupies himself with dirty magazines and self-abuse, is going to give us his instant opinion of how we're conducting ourselves – through a megaphone. 'Hands out of your pockets Miggins!'

And because the health fascists are getting ever more strident every day, no doubt it's only a question of time before they will be screaming their strictures at the people they think are too fat, or too thin, are smoking a cigarette or need a bloody haircut.

So that's what has pissed me off this morning – or more accurately, it's just one of the things. You don't need me to tell you that you don't want to know about all the others.

All of which bollocks brings me to the big question and the concluding question which Grumpy Old Men would ask in relation to our subject, and it's this. Why is it that we have to go to work at all? What is it about the human condition that we all assume that we have to go to work?

Your immediate reaction to this is that the answer is obvious. We have to eat, we have to keep warm and sure we need to have somewhere to lay our heads. But just think about it for a minute. These have been basic needs since before the Fall. (No, I don't mean before the autumn; we aren't all Americans – yet.) For most of the period since the end of the Garden of Eden, satisfying those basic human needs has been a question of obtaining food and keeping the rain off. Our ancestors were hunter-gatherers, we're told, tracking down the baby brontosaurus and bringing it back to be placed inside two pieces of pitta bread for a little light supper. A sort of pre-historic doner kebab but without the salmonella. Simple and to the point. You hunted, or you starved.

Then we were farmers, turning over the soil, growing our own stuff, making our own bread to eat and beer to drink. To put a roof over our heads, maybe we were hollowing out the cave or knocking together some old driftwood. Then we were putting a few pelts down on the hard rock to take the weight off our feet or to ease our careworn tushies so that we could enjoy an episode of *The Generation Game* in comfort – or whatever was the contemporary equivalent. Whatever it was, I'm sure Bruce Forsyth was in it. Basic stuff. All good natural activity which goes directly towards providing ourselves with food and shelter in a way that you can sort of get your head around.

But here's the thing about it. All of this activity was very directly designed to provide for our most basic needs, to keep us alive and ticking, presumably so that we could get on with our lives. It was all a means to an end. Work was the means, living was the end. You know – living – the other things we did, whatever they were, when we were not working to enable ourselves to do them. See?

I mean stuff like read a book, play an instrument, play with the kids, walk through the forest, talk about the universe, complain about the weather. You know the sort of thing – it's called living.

This was the original work-life balance. Feed yourself and the kids, make sure you were all warm enough, and then get on with stuff. Do enough work to enable yourself and your dependents to live. The combination so beloved of those original advertisements for Mars bars.

So the question I and other Grumpies would want to ask these days is: how did we get from there, doing natural things to provide for our basic human needs for as much time as it took to secure them, all the way to a situation where work has actually become our reason to be? All the way from our more or less natural state, to a situation where we find ourselves sitting in a little booth for eight hours a day wearing a headset and making telephone calls to people we've never heard of and who don't want to hear from us, asking them if they would like to participate in a survey? Or sitting in front of a silver screen all day looking at the prices of 'futures' whatever they may be. Or at a conveyer belt.

Exactly how did we get from 'I'm hungry, how can I get myself a cheese and pickle sandwich?' or 'I'm tired, I wonder if I can find myself a bit of soft moss somewhere', to a point where many or most of us are sacrificing the most precious and irrecoverable thing we all have – our time – to a range of activities so mindless, heartless, soul-less, moronic and pointless? And so all-consuming.

Exactly how did we find ourselves persuaded to make these asinine activities so much the centre of our lives, that pretty much everything else goes out of the window to make way for them?

We don't just dedicate that part of our lives that we have to in order to eat and thrive, and then spend the rest of our time enjoying ourselves; we spend more or less all of our 'disposable time' at work, leaving ourselves hardly any time at all to do the things that we are earning the money to make possible. Do you see what I mean? The merits of 'work, rest and play' have been substituted by all those addictive energy drinks which mean you can go on working for longer, and longer, and longer. Or, if you work in the City, by all those regular snorts of cocaine.

Rather than something we do in order to enable us to live our lives, work has *become* our lives. It defines us, and if you doubt what I'm saying, ask yourself how long you can stand and talk to someone you don't know at a party before one or other of you says 'and what do you do?' About two and a half minutes max, I'd guess, and when he asks that question, he's not asking you what job you do; he's asking what you *are*.

So that, if you say 'I am an architect', he'll say, 'that must be interesting' and you'll start to talk about what you have designed recently, and you'll both go on talking about it until it's time to stop talking altogether. If he says 'I am in advertising' all of a sudden you know where to place him in the hierarchy which has replaced class in modern Britain. He's better than a policeman but probably not as good as a barrister. Got you taped, we can all relax. You know what he is.

What is more, as soon as you know what he does, you can feel free to make all your assumptions about where he is in relation to you. If you ask him what he does and he says 'I'm a salesman', that's probably fine unless you are also a salesman. In that case, you've got to get the measure of him in relation to yourself so you are going to have to ask what it is that he sells. If he says 'computer salesman' and you work in a shoe store, you're probably going to have to hear all his anecdotes because his job will be presumed to be more interesting than yours, and so he'll be thought to be a more interesting person than you.

Just by the way, those of us who work in the media are more guilty of this than anyone. Because we work in telly, we think the chances are that we're the most interesting of anyone in the room, so we can't wait for someone to ask us what we do. Then, with or without the slightest encouragement, we will go on for ages about what it is we do and how we do it, usually taking the opportunity to drop in the fact that we met Jeremy Clarkson or Jonathan Ross at some industry event only this week. (This usually means that we didn't actually 'meet' them, we saw them at a distance, waved, but they didn't really recognise us and so just smiled.)

We in the media are the worst of the worst, and the only thing to be said in our defence is that others encourage us. 'Oh really, that must be fascinating.' 'Oh do you think so? Well yes, as a matter of fact it is. Why only today …' and then we're off.

Actually, now I come to think about it, we're not quite the worst of the worst. Lawyers are pretty bad at this and so, as I mention it, are architects, but the actual worst of the worst – and if you've ever experienced this you'll agree with me like a shot – are politicians. Politicians are without peer the worst of the worst at assuming that what they do is so much more fascinating than anything that anyone else could possibly do. And they want to go on and on and on and on about it.

But entrancing though all this is, we've strayed a little way off the point, which was that we define ourselves by what we do rather than by what we are. We're a plumber, not a husband; a car dealer not a dad; we're a farmer, not a fly-fisherman.

Which would be sort of OK if we enjoyed it – if work was the point of living, but for most of us it isn't. For most of us work is a means of living, not the end, but we spend an utterly disproportionate amount of our time on it. Which leaves no time for anything else, and so that after a while we forget that there is even supposed to be anything else. Work has become our lives. Which makes Grumpy people Grumpy.

Somehow we've all been persuaded that we need to do all this utterly pointless stuff in order to keep body and soul together, but if you think for a moment about it, you'll realise that it isn't actually necessary for us to do all this alien activity to feed and clothe ourselves, is it? We've found a couple of times in the last century that it's possible for just about every able-bodied man in the country to stop doing anything productive and go off and do precisely the opposite, for years at a time, and we all somehow managed to continue to eat, sleep and clothe ourselves. And do you know what? Before it's finally too late to get the chance, ask a survivor of World War Two what was the happiest time of his or her life, and as likely as not I think you'll find that they'll say 'during the war'. The reason they give is because 'we all pulled together'. All around them bombs were dropping and innocents were dying, but this was the happiest time of their lives because 'we were all pulling together'.

So it turns out that our basic happiness is not about working hard at school and getting a job which has all the appeal and effect of formaldehyde poured though a hole in the ear-drum. It turns out that happiness is about feeling a sense of community, and where does achieving a sense of community figure in our list of priorities?

No, between us it seems that we've created a society where maintaining a decent standard of living in which we can work, rest and play is not enough. We have continually to be pushing, and pressing, and trying to 'get on'. Our consumer-driven society demands it of us, and so we just cannot afford to relax. We've got to devote the vast majority of our time and energy to it, and to work our tails off in the process.

The French had a go at getting this right a few years ago – they enforced the thirty-five-hour week and made it very difficult to fire anybody. As a result they had a reasonable work-life balance during normal times, and in August they all took the entire month off and buggered off to the countryside. A friend of mine who lives in France told me that he always knows how to get hold of the plumber or the electrician or the carpenter – he just waits until lunchtime and phones him at home; he is always there having his lunch.

But of course that couldn't work could it? Why? Because the rest of us are so mad that we are still working all the hours that God made. The French could have their simple and straightforward and civilised work-life balance, but the price they would have to pay is that every other European economy would overtake them in terms of overall prosperity. Because we are all working forty or fifty or sixty hours a week, and they are not.

So they've had to give it up. They've elected a President whose manifesto actually said he was going to make their lives tougher. Though they have plenty to eat and drink, live in very nice houses and take nice long holidays in their beautiful countryside, that's not enough. Doing well is only OK if no-one else is doing better. You can only have a life if everyone else also settles for having a life.

Meanwhile, back in Britain we've made a life for ourselves in which we are all like pathetic little hamsters on a treadmill, running just to stand still, and the faster we run, the faster life becomes a blur until eventually we will drop down dead without ever really getting the chance to learn what it was all about. The whole system is set up so that we have to keep running, and so that most of us will never get anywhere.

It can't be that bad? You think? Well let's do the basic arithmetic.

I believe that the average salary for a working man in Britain as I write is about £27,000 a year. It's a long time since I've had a proper job, but I'm guessing that after tax, national insurance or whatever, this ends up as about £18,000 in the pocket. There or thereabouts. If our salary earner has to go to work by car, with depreciation, road tax, insurance, MOT and fuel, you can deduct at least £3,000 a year, taking that to £15,000. Going to work on public transport is going to have a very similar effect. If he or she also lives and works in London and needs the car to go to work, that's another £2,000 a year at least for the congestion charge, leaving £13,000. If he or she also has to park the car in a big city, that could easily be another £5,000 a year, but let's assume that's prohibitive and call it £1,000 a year, leaving this person with £12,000. I don't know what it costs to eat, but let's assume a minimum of £50 a week per person, which is £2,500 a year leaving £8,500 if this person lives alone and £6,000 if he/she is supporting just one other person. Gas, electricity, water rates, council tax, has got to be another £3,500 a year leaving £2,500. Life insurance? Pension contributions? Annual holiday? Let's say £2,000 leaving £500. Clothes? Must be at least £20 a week averaged across the year, which is £1,000 leaving minus £500. TV licence? New telly every five years or so? And so on and so on …

So that's how the average annual salary of the average working person in Britain goes from £27,000 down to less than nothing, and has anyone noticed the thing I've missed out? Apart from the other costs associated with any dependents, I mean? Oh yes, I've missed out the biggest thing of all. The mortgage.

The mortgage alone, on a two-bedroom flat in south-west London where we live, would wipe out the entire disposable income of this average person before they even got to the next item. At the time of writing, a two-bedroom flat in our neighbourhood costs about £250,000, the mortgage on which at (let's say) 6% would be £15,000 a year, and with council tax and property insurance that'll wipe out the whole take-home pay of the average worker.

What follows is we've made it impossible for a family living in some parts of the country to live at all unless both adults are working, which means that the entire life's output of one of the two working people in the household is dedicated to maintaining a roof over the head of the family. Just think about that. The idea of having to work for eight hours a day, five days a week, for forty-eight weeks out of fifty-two, just so that you can live in a two-bedroom flat. How can that make sense?

And the particular irony is that, somehow or other, many of us have persuaded ourselves that we're lucky that property is so expensive. We regard it as part of our wealth, and feel rather superior to the French or Italians in whose countries we seem to be able to buy relative palaces for the same as it would cost to buy a semi-detached garage in Altringham or Poole.

We leave to one side the fact that these riches are entirely notional, because for them to be turned into anything we could spend we would have to sell up, trade down or make ourselves homeless. It just makes us feel good. We're 'millionaires', apparently, if our houses are worth a million pounds, simply ignoring the fact that – as a consequence of having a mortgage of the size necessary to live in them – we can't afford to go out to dinner!

So which ones of us are the idiots? Is it the French or the Italians or the Spanish, for whom the cost of their accommodation is a significant but not crippling part of their living expenses, or the bloody gullible idiotic British who have to work our tails off for all the hours that God made, just to be able to live with a roof and four walls? I think I know the answer.

How did we get ourselves into this situation? How did we get all the way from a position in which we had to secure our own food – by hunting or growing it, and maintain a shelter over our heads with our own hands, and had a little bit of time and energy left over to live, all the way to a situation in which we now sacrifice our entire lives in exchange for what we should regard as the very basics of living?

We could blame the estate agents for constantly talking up the price of property to a level where ordinary folk have to worry themselves sick about how to meet the payments. We could blame the politicians who sold off council houses and have never delivered on decades of promises to build what is euphemistically called 'affordable housing'. Some of us might even blame ourselves for putting up with it.

But of course in the end the answer is a combination of all of those and more. The answer is that it's all about 'the man'. Work in general, and work like this in particular, was invented by 'the man' to keep the rest of us in check. Because if we didn't spend our time engaged in utterly useless and ultimately unrewarding activity, chances are that we might have time to ask a few more profound questions. Questions that have historically got quite a few people into trouble. Questions like 'how come you get to own the factory and I don't?' Or 'how come you get to own the land and I don't?' Or 'how come I work in the factory and you work in the office, but you earn 100 times what I earn?' Or 'why do I have to work all of my life just to be able to put a roof over our heads?'

So in order to prevent us from asking those kinds of questions, which can only lead to dissent and all sorts of undesirable stuff, our lives had to be organised for us. Society had to be arranged so that we are obliged to fall into line, work hard at school, get an education, get some skills, get a job, so we can spend the rest of our lives paying the mortgage. And if somewhere along the line we fall outside of the system; if the wheels fall off somewhere because the old man leaves home or the old lady suffers from depression or we get in with the wrong crowd, we're up shit-creek. No job, no money, no integration into the machine, and we're one of the millions of kids and young adults we see in every major town and city in the country living like outlaws or feral beasts in what we used to call 'the black economy'.

Where do you think all this depressing polemic is leading? Well of course to the fact that we're Grumpy. We're Grumpy about everything in general, and we're Grumpy about the whole wide world of work in particular. We've helped to create a world which has turned us into the very automatons which were supposed to make us free, and we're pissed off about it. So we're Grumpy Old Men and we're Grumpy Old Women.

Does all this stuff make you fucking sick, or what?